D1325598

Crocodiles in the Fernery, Pelicans in the Pond

Crocodiles in the Fernery, Pelicans in the Pond

Histories of entertaining and
unlikely garden pets

Twigs Way

Illustrations by Phillip Bentley

SUTTON PUBLISHING

First published in the United Kingdom in 2008 by
The History Press
Cirencester Road · Chalford · Stroud · Gloucestershire · GL6 8PE

British Library Cataloguing in Publication Data
A catalogue record for this book is available from the British Library.

ISBN 978 0 7509 4872 2

Typesetting and origination by
The History Press
Printed and bound in England.

This book is dedicated to
Bramble (1999–2006), Parsnip (1999–2007) and Sage (2004–2007)
for whom the whole world was a garden; and to
Sweet Pea, Blackberry, Pumpkin, Damson, Quince, Mulberry, Bluebell,
Teasel, Willow and Robinia,
who continue their work of destruction.

Acknowledgements

As ever, this book could not have been written without the assistance of a great many people. Of those who responded to my pleas for information I would like to especially thank the following: Caroline Holmes for being a constant fount of information; Nicola Campbell for her information on Devon sites and the emu-loving, eccentric Peek family in particular; Linden Groves for allowing me access to her MA dissertation on 'Animals: Living Garden Features Not Incidental Occupants'; Robin Loder of Leonardslee for sharing his childhood with the wallabies; Patrick Phillips of Kentwell Hall for the entry on doves; Elizabeth Johnson for the history of the ducks at Cambridge University Library (and for the care she took in raising them); Susie Pasley-Tyler of Coton Manor for the history of the flamingos there; Jill Raggett of Writtle College for her advice on Japanese Gardens and goldfish; Andrew Widd (then at English Heritage) on the otter at Audley End; Sam Youd, Head Gardener at Tatton Park, on tree frogs; Karen Wisemen, Education Officer at Blenheim Palace; Ros Wallinger for her comments on Jack the donkey at Munstead Wood; and Kate Fielden, archivist at Bowood for very kindly leading me away from the lures of the orang-utan in the Orangery!

'Sir, to leave things out of a book, merely because people tell you they will not be believed, is meanness'
Dr Samuel Johnson quoted in James Boswell's *Life of Johnson* vol. 2

Introduction

'Let there be shade and let the windows of the pavilion look out upon the garden. Let fish-pools be made and diverse fishes placed therein. Let there also be hares, rabbits, deer and such-like wild animals that are not beasts of prey. And in the trees near the pavilion let great cages be made and therein place partridges, nightingales, blackbirds, linnets and all manner of singing birds. Let all be arranged so that the beasts and the birds may be easily seen from the pavilion'. So said Petrius Crescentius in his early fourteenth century Italian text on estate and garden management. Petrius was not to know that the fashion for introducing birds and beasts into the garden was already a long established one by the time of his writing, nor that it would still be alive and well in the twenty-first century. From the Mesopotamian kings who created parks, or *paradesios*, to house the animals of tribute brought to them, to the wallabies that still wander free in a twenty-first century Sussex garden, our parks and gardens have been enlivened by cries, calls and capers, as fauna join flora in delighting the human soul. Some creatures of course enliven more than others. Snaileries can never produce the same frisson as the presence of an elephant, whilst however charming a flock of demoiselle cranes, a single striped hyena prowling the lawn (even when called 'Squeak') will inevitably command more attention.

Down the centuries it would seem almost every conceivable type of beast, bird and fish have been kept as garden animals. Large or small, tame or wild, timid or terrifying, someone somewhere has attempted to integrate it into their horticultural schema. In his idyllic fourteenth century Garden of Love, Chaucer imagines hares and rabbits, timid deer, squirrels and all beasts of gentle kind, excluding only beasts of prey and the much maligned frog. The Reverend Theodore Wood, Victorian clergyman and naturalist, would have empathised with Chaucer, specialising as he did in keeping only those animals (and insects) that were native to this country. With a fernery full of toads, and a conservatory of glow-worms, the Reverend Theodore had no recourse to the importation of exotic animals. The Angora rabbit held no charms for the Reverend, whilst the humble guinea pig did not move him to even passing admiration. For others, the delight in all things natural combined perfectly with the challenge of the collector, and for several centuries menageries of exotic birds and beasts became a hallmark of any nobleman's park or garden. Unusual and diverse collections demonstrated both the intellect and power of their owners, who might command the abduction of animals from newly discovered lands, paying vast sums for their global transportation. But even amongst these collections, individual attachments might be made, especially where an animal was more than usually long-lived. Menageries also had a way of growing, such that what might start as a small collection or individual specimen placed discretely in one part of a private pleasure ground, all too easily grew to invade the rest of the gardens, with bears in the summerhouse and tree frogs in the fernery.

For the less well-off, or those lacking the collectors' zeal, animal care was a more personal affair. The animals collected up into these personal Edens would be prized not for their uncommonness, or perhaps we should say not just for their uncommonness, but also as individuals. Ranging from the cute and malleable to the downright ugly and vicious, these individuals would roam freely the gardens and pleasure grounds, and in some cases even into the houses of their owners. In the case of W.S. Gilbert's cuddly lemurs, this presented no difficulties for even the most timorous visitor, but surely a crocodile, or even an over-affectionate capybara, might introduce barriers to neighbourly social intercourse. In fact neighbourly relations could be severely strained by the very presence of these animals. The artist Dante Gabriel Rossetti was bombarded with complaints from his wealthy London neighbours over his tunnelling armadillo and his discordant peacocks. Although no-one appears to have had the temerity to complain to Emperor Charlemagne about his elephant.

Not all of the animals in this book, or in the history of the garden, are rare or exotic or even dangerous. Sentimentality towards the 'lesser creatures' increased enormously in the Victorian period and cats, dogs, rabbits and guinea pigs (not to mention salamanders, lizards, toads, monkeys and others) held sway over many households by the end of the nineteenth century. Gertrude Jekyll, that great Surrey gardener, was so inordinately fond of cats that she devoted an entire chapter to them in one of her many gardening books, whilst her contemporary William Robinson looked on fondly as his dog, Boy, crushed an entire bed of his prize-winning tufted pansies. William Cowper was lost without his hares, and the Reverend Wood entertained his neighbours by imitating the walk of his much loved chameleon. Even exotics might become naturalised, and the setting up of the original London Zoological Gardens (note the word 'gardens'!) owed much to the imperialist aim of 'acclimatising' a range of animals and birds to the climate of England. Once adapted, these ornaments could be of practical and decorative utility to country gentlemen in their gardens, parks and farms. The original design of the zoo was in the favoured landscape style of the time, mingling garden features with *ferme ornée*. Alas, as so many gardeners and pet-lovers have discovered, the battle between *ferme* and *ornée* is one that ornament is destined to lose in all but the largest gardens, and the site needed continual re-planting.

The early twentieth century saw, if anything, a rise in the numbers of people who shared their gardens with the sort of wildlife not usually envisaged by modern 'wildlife gardeners'. No longer the preserve of the wealthy, exotic animals were seen in even middle-class establishments and gardens. Rather than crested newts and bird feeders, the seventy members of the Amateur Menagerie Club introduced monkeys and beaver dens. A short lived society (1912–1927) of men and women, the club's yearbook is full of the joys of keeping individual animals of all types as pets. One typical article commences 'A crocodile is distinctly an unconventional pet, and one likely to draw down remark and criticism upon the taste and judgement of the owner, but, in common with all reptiles, he has much to recommend him'. Similarly enthusiastic praises can be found in modern books on the keeping of unusual pets in house and garden. In 2007 the usual has become the unusual, as books appear on pot-bellied pigs, salamanders, and rats.

What next, one is forced to ask, *Hermit Crabs for Dummies*?

As an exploration of individual animals, 'pets' and those in small collections, this book largely avoids the history of the larger menagerie and eschews the zoo. One or two favoured animals may have crept in from the larger collections of royalty or nobility, but only where they appear to have been favoured by their owners or carers beyond the usual. This book is then both a tribute and a fond remembrance of all those who have stood by watching whilst cats uproot the catnip, rabbits prune the fruit trees and tree frogs spit venom amongst the ferns. Whilst there are still those that follow Petrius Crescentius in his love of flora and fauna combined there will always be gardens where the hyena and the hellebore mix, crocodiles inhabit the fernery and there are pelicans in the pond.

Author's Note:

On the theory that most readers will wish to turn to B for bear or W for wallaby rather than chase the Latin classification of U for *Ursus* and M for *Macropus* (except of course when they are D for *Dorcopsis*!) this book has been arranged using common English names. In many instances there is not enough information to surmise which varieties or sub-species of animals were kept, and in early days most owners would either not have known or not have cared. After all, an elephant is a pretty impressive garden pet whichever the species! Therefore in the admirably appropriate words of Mrs R Lee, in her 1852 book *Anecdotes of the Habits and Instinct of Animals* 'Dry details of science and classification have been laid aside, but a certain order has been kept to avoid confusion'.

The Gardener and the Hog

A gard'ner, of peculiar taste,
On a young hog his favour placed;
Who fed not with the common herd;
His tray was to the hall preferred.
He wallowed underneath the board,
Or in his master's chamber snored;
Who fondly stroked him every day,
And taught him all the puppy's play;
Where'er he went, the grunting friend
Ne'er failed his pleasure to attend.

As on a time, the loving pair
Walked forth to tend the garden's care,
The master thus address'd the swine:
 'My house, my garden, all is thine.
On turnips feast whene'er you please,
And riot in my beans and peas;
If the potato's taste delights,
Or the red carrot's sweet invites,
Indulge thy morn and evening hours,
But let due care regard my flowers:

My tulips are my garden's pride,
What vast expense those beds supplied!'
The hog by chance one morning roamed,
Where with new ale the vessels foamed.
He munches now the steaming grains,
Now with full swill the liquor drains.
Intoxicating fumes arise;

He reels, he rolls his winking eyes;
Then stagg'ring through the garden scours,
And treads down painted ranks of flowers.

With delving snout he turns the soil,
And cools his palate with the spoil.
The master came, the ruin spied,
'Villain, suspend thy rage,' he cried.
'Hast thou, thou most ungrateful sot,
My charge, my only charge forgot?
What, all my flowers!' No more he said,
But gazed, and sighed, and hung his head.
The hog with stutt'ring speech returns:
'Explain, sir, why your anger burns.

See there, untouched, your tulips strown,
For I devoured the roots alone.'
At this the gard'ner's passion grows;
From oaths and threats he fell to blows.
The stubborn brute the blow sustains;
Assaults his leg, and tears the veins.
Ah! foolish swain, too late you find
That sties were for such friends designed!
Homeward he limps with painful pace,
Reflecting thus on past disgrace:

Who cherishes a brutal mate
Shall mourn the folly soon or late.

John Gay 1727
Fable XLVIII

ALPACA

The donkey and the camel are the traditional beasts associated with the Christmas story, a story not notable for any garden setting, but at Barrow, Suffolk, the age old story is given a rather different twist with the aid of three alpacas. Balthazar, Melchior and Caspar spend most of their days quietly munching grass in the idyllic gardens of The Rectory under the watchful eye of Father Peter Macleod Miller. In a truly Christian manner they share their pasturage with two donkeys, a handful of sheep, some rather upmarket hens and an obstreperous goat called Margaret. However come Christmas they throw aside both their South American roots and their quiet retirement and make the journey to the nearby ancient pilgrimage town of Bury St Edmunds. Here they take on the role of kingly camels in the 'Living Nativity' perform-ance that draws in the surrounding parishes and the people of Bury St. Edmunds. In a makeshift stable, in the otherwise commercial Christmas market, the ecumenical menagerie create an oasis of gentle lowing, baaing and clucking amongst the buying and selling. Palm Sunday again sees them lured away from their Garden of Eden into the wider world, to add a uniquely cross-continental view of the Christian story. Their normally quiet months of retire-ment have not however been without their upsets. One summer's day, in the long recess between public appear-ances, Melchior was found lying stiff and motionless in the Rectory garden. A local, retired, vet was called, whose practice used to be in Scotland. Seeing the immediacy of the emergency, he called for whisky, and with great care he slipped the amber liquid down Melchior's throat. Apparently in the remoter wilds of Scotland fifty or sixty years ago whisky was sometimes the only readily available medicine, and was often used with great effect. Certainly the alpaca staged a miraculous recovery and has never looked back. Fortunately, Melchior and his supporting cast are not from a teetotal sect.

ARMADILLO

In his 1607 *Historie of Four Footed Beastes*, the English cleric Edward Topsell recorded that the merchantmen and citizens of London kept armadillos (then known as 'the Guinean Beast') and fed them on garden earth-worms. Perhaps inspired by this precedent, the Victorian painter Dante Gabriel Rossetti decided that he too would have a pair of armadillos in his garden at Cheyne Walk, London. Convinced that the creatures were harmless to all, he allowed them the full freedom of the garden, where they proceeded to disabuse him of this notion by creating a trail of destruction. Although Rossetti's own garden appears by then to have had little worth destroy-ing – much already having been eaten by the wombats, racoon and peacocks – his long-suffering neighbours still clung to some horticultural remnants, and it was to these that the armadillos turned their attention. Armadillos are constructed with excavation in mind. Short stout legs, strong claws, long tapered bodies, and armour plating, enable them to rapidly transform flower-beds and lawn into a series of trenches in their search for insect and plant titbits.

As Harry Dunn, Rossetti's artistic assistant, recalled, 'Now and then our neighbour's garden would be found to have large heaps of earth thrown up, and some of his choicest plants lying waste over the beds. This was the work of the armadillos'. One even managed to tunnel through to the floor of a neighbouring basement kitchen. When the hysteria subsided, the cook was heard to exclaim 'If it isn't the Devil, there is no knowing what it is'. In desperation Rossetti's neighbour attempted to poison the beasts with beef saturated with prussic acid, but after an absence of three months, the armadillos suddenly re-appeared. Looking sadly mangy and 'out at the elbows' the armadillos had (literally) gone underground in an attempt to avoid early death, and lived for several months on grubs and beetles in relative retirement. Unfortunately they did not appear to have learnt their lesson, and were soon wreaking havoc again through the gardens of Cheyne Walk. Fortunately for Rossetti's neighbours he was made to see horticultural sense, and the armadillos were eventually handed over to the London Zoological Gardens. In fact Rossetti's fascination with animals had commenced in childhood with visits to this establishment, which had inspired him to 'adopt' a dormouse and a 'hedgehog of unpredictable behaviour'. It was lucky for all on Cheyne Walk that Rossetti's penchant for an elephant to replace the armadillo was never fulfilled, although a much longed for wombat did eventually join the merry gardening throng (and can be found under W).

ASSAPANICK

On 26 July 1788 William Thornton, American physician and architect of the U.S. Capitol, wrote the following to Dr Lettsom, English amateur botanist. 'I have sent you four assapanick or flying squirrels and four ground squirrels. The flying squirrels are a family, male and female, with two young ones; the young are very easily tamed; the ladies here have them running all over them, and carry them in their pockets or bosoms, with a small collar of leather round their necks, and a little chain. They do not bite, but soon grow familiar. The old ones and ground squirrels are more difficult, but may, by constantly handling them in gloves, be tamed. You may keep the old, male and female, of the flying variety, and one of each sort of the ground, to breed.' Lettsom took his correspondent at his word and installed the squirrels in his large Surrey garden as a delight to his visitors, friends and family. Here they joined his tortoises, pyramidal bee-houses, and the collection of mangle-worzels that this eccentric man was attempting to introduce into England. The assapanick were apparently a success in their new home and word spread of these charming and hardy pets. Fifty years later the fellows of the Zoological Society were recording that there was no creature 'more graceful, or one better fitted for a lady's pet'. Its diminutive size, the singularity of its form, the expression of its physiognomy, the vivacity of its motions, and the gentleness of its disposition all combine to render it one of the most interesting as one of the most beautiful'. Lady's pet or not, President Theodore Roosevelt also took to the assapanick, continuing the tradition set by Dr Lettsom by allowing the creatures run of the house and gardens.

AXOLOTL

Not content with admiring his father's crocodile pond (see C for Crocodile), the young Harry Boyle at Eller How in the Lake District kept axolotl, a type of salamander. Looking back in his later years he recalled the wonders of watching these strange amphibians seemingly turn from fish to reptiles, changing colours, looks and habit as they moved through the garden. Now he thought, he had them safe in the pond; and lo and behold the next day they had all turned white and were scuttling about the bushes in the garden, forever getting lost and having to be found. According to his wife and biographer the axolotl were his cherished pets. Each were named and each tamed, although how one tames a free-ranging axolotl is a mystery!

BABOON

Unlike their counterparts in early zoos and travelling shows, animals in private gardens and collections were rarely subjected to the unreliable actions of the public. However the unfortunate 'Man Tyger' which formed part of the small royal collection in the eighteenth century appears to have created an exception in the normally polite reactions of the upper-class visitors to the establishment. On sighting strangers he would 'heave any thing within his reach' at them, and they would in turn 'heave' it back. Perhaps more dextrous than his human opponents he would apparently catch anything so flung at him. His dextrousness took another turn when women approached as he was lecherous to a 'surprising degree' and would, in the words of polite contemporaries, 'make motions' of his desires'. His youth was taken as an excuse for such indecorous behaviour, although whether he grew out of it is not recorded. An older and less sexually indiscrete baboon in the same royal collection also had the unfortunate habit of 'heaving' various objects at passers-by. Included within the list of his weapons were stones, stools, bowls, and even a canon shot of nine pounds in weight, the last having killed a cabin boy during the sea journey over. Baboons apparently do not make good cruise companions. Royal hospitality seemed to have improved his manners slightly, and this older baboon would, at times, sit on a stool rather than throwing it. Both baboons were reported as behaving with actions 'nearly approaching to the human species', although as this included throwing objects, fighting and masturbating it seems to reflect poorly on eighteenth century London society. Lechery is a theme in the history of baboons in close contact with humans, as a specimen at Chester was recorded by the eighteenth century naturalist Thomas Pennant as also being excessively libidinous.

BABOON II

In his diary entry for 16 August 1872, the nineteenth century parson Francis Kilvert noted that 'the baboon at Maesllwch Castle' had full run of both the gardens and castle itself. It had chased his neighbours the Baskervilles, who, in mortal fear, were forced to put spurs to their horses to outrun the baboon as it chased them out of the grounds. When not seeing off visitors, the baboon occupied its time carrying cats to the highest tower and dropping them off. Kilvert firmly believed that it was only a matter of time before it carried out the same deed with the young heir to the castle.

BADGER

The naturalist Frances Pitt (1888–1964) kept a wide variety of animals, mostly native wildlife that had been abandoned or orphaned. Many of these lived in her study or her attic (a most appropriate place for her bats), but Diana and Jemima Muggins, her pet badgers, found a home in her garden. Badgers taken as adults never made satisfactory pets according to Frances, but Diana and Jemima had been rescued as cubs after their mother had been trapped and killed. Fortunately old enough to have been weaned, the six-week-olds arrived hungry, frightened and very angry. It might have been any of these three emotions which caused them to bite into everything within reach on their arrival, but Miss Pitt had the naturalist's instinct and the proffering of freshly killed rabbit soon satisfied everyone, except the rabbit. The two badgers were found a home in an old pigsty, once so common in country gardens, and fed on a diet of dog biscuits, kitchen scraps, and dead rats (also once common in country gardens). Diana was the tamest of the two and would follow Frances around like a dog, whimpering to be picked up and carried when her short legs became tired, quickly learning to sit up and beg to be carried on these daily outings. As a baby this presented no problems, but dead rats and dog biscuits soon resulted in a considerably weightier burden for Miss Pitt. When out in the garden the badgers would play with the dogs; a retriever, a terrier, and a spaniel named Geff (*sic.*) with whom Diana would roll on the ground, chase, snort, and run in circles, before collapsing in an exhausted heap. Strangers made the sisters nervous and Diana would hide under Frances Pitt's skirts, or if indoors when they called, under the furniture, from where she was very difficult to extract. From her sub-furnishings den she would sally forth only to offers of cake or thin bread and butter, but once alone with the family Diana would sit comfortably on the armchairs. The outside world still called to Diana and Jemima's hearts however, and their walks around the garden and down the lane must have stirred a longing for freedom. One summer's evening Diana slipped her lead and disappeared into the shrubbery. From the shrubbery to the wilderness is a short journey, whether horticulturally or literally, and Diana was soon living wild in the woods again. Taking sympathy on the remaining sister, Frances Pitt took Jemima to her native Shropshire woods and let her free. Badgers were obviously once relatively common pets, as the Amateur Menagerie Club (of whom Frances was a member) declared that there were few of its members who did not keep a badger or otter.

BEAR

When Dr John Coakley Lettsom moved to Camberwell (Surrey) in 1779 it was, according to the parish records, a parish plagued by caterpillars, hedgehogs and sparrows. Dr Lettsom's arrival at his especially commissioned house, Grove Hill, added an air of exoticism to the parish's burdens with his collection of flying squirrels, a great white American owl, and an escaping bear. Primarily a physician, plant collector and botanist, Lettsom exchanged plants and seeds with his contacts throughout England, Europe, America, India and the East Indies. Amongst these were the famous William Curtis, founder of *Curtis' Botanical Magazine*; Dr Fothergill, the plant collector from Upton House, Essex, and most importantly, William Thornton, a fellow Quaker and anti-slave campaigner from the West Indies resident in America whilst promoting his schemes for independent colonies. Thornton occupied his 'spare' time from his campaigning by collecting and sending plants over from America to his botanical contacts in England. As a Quaker, Lettsom had a more than usual interest in the natural world created by God for the sober use and improvement of man, and he was anxious to collect examples not just of America's flora but also its fauna. In his letter to Thornton concerning the botanic collections, Lettsom thus requested 'some true original American turkies'. Perhaps turkeys were in short supply, for what Thornton sent was an owl and a bear. The bear arrived safely and Lettsom installed him in the garden at Grove Hill amongst the American shrub borders, the Conservatory, the marble statue of Cupid, and the stone tablet inscribed with the praise of all God's manifold works. Lettsom described the new acquisition to his garden as 'remarkably playful', probably an understatement for a bear which finally found itself free and on stable ground again after several weeks in a small cage with seasickness. Frequently slipping his collar the bear afforded 'considerable diversion' to Lettsom and his servants as they attempted to recapture him in the large grounds. His periods of liberty grew longer and more frequent as he learnt to give his captors the slip, and he grew predictably vicious at attempts to recapture him. Urged by his Camberwell neighbours to rid the parish of this unexpected burden Lettsom kindly offered him to his friend Pickering, who wisely declined, fearful of any incidents with his children from keeping a bear in his own garden.

Lettsom himself had six children, but does not seem to have felt that was a restriction to the keeping of wild animals. The somewhat more secure accommodation at the Tower menagerie was unfortunately already home to two other bears and so Lettsom was forced to keep him. Finally the bear managed to again escape into the neighbourhood and, defying capture for two days this time, did 'no little mischief'. Local feeling ran high in the small village and Lettsom was forced to allow the bear to be killed. Later he blamed the bear's unpredictable moods on the circumstance of its being female, and requested that in future Thornton should only send him male animals; although this must have been a hindrance to his stated aim of setting up breeding colonies of animals likely to be 'useful' in some way to the English economy.

BEAR II

Some of the most famous gardens in the world have been the homes of unusual pets, and the White House (USA) is no exception. As well as the wide range of pets kept by President Lincoln, (see T for Turkey) and President Coolidge (see R for Raccoon), Theodore Roosevelt made the presidential house and grounds a home for a lizard named Bill; guinea pigs named Admiral Dewey, Dr. Johnson, Bishop Doane, Fighting Bob Evans, and Father O'Grady; Maude the pig; Josiah the badger; Eli Yale the blue macaw; Baron Spreckle the hen; a one-legged rooster; a hyena; a barn owl; Peter the rabbit; and Algonquin the pony. However, his most famous garden pet was a bear called Jonathan Edwards. As he explained in a letter dated 22 November 1900: 'Some of my Republican supporters in West Virginia have just sent me a small bear which the children of

their own accord christened Jonathan Edwards, partly out of compliment to their mother's ancestor, and partly because they thought they detected Calvinistic traits in the bear's character.' Bear and children played happily in the garden (despite any Calvinistic traits) before the bear was eventually gifted to a zoo. It has to be wondered whether sending a live bear to someone is necessarily an indication of personal or political support! Roosevelt of course became famous for inspiring the popularity of the 'Teddy Bear' as a result of refusing to shoot a black bear encountered on a hunting trip. Perhaps he was remembering Jonathan Edwards?

BEAR III

In the 1860s, a small rustic summerhouse in the gardens of Killerton, Devon, became the home of a pet black bear. Brought back from Canada by the well-travelled Gilbert Acland, son of the 11th Baronet Thomas Acland, the bear was for some reason thought to be an appropriate inmate for the house, with its adjoining pool. Replete with thatched roof, stone steps, and stained glass windows, the summerhouse still remains, although the bear is long gone. Proving both a scourge and a delight to the neighbourhood, the bear was eventually sent packing to the London Zoological Gardens, whose cages, one fears, did not boast stained glass. In the same period another pet bear was kept in the game larder at Shadwell Park, Norfolk. What exactly it was doing there, and whether this combined use of carnivore house and game larder was successful is unrecorded.

BEAVER

Some animals, although initially welcomed into the house find themselves banished to the garden as a result of their unusual and often inconvenient habits (inconvenient that is in the eyes of the human inhabitants). Binny the beaver however found his way determinedly from the garden into the house despite a range of behaviour that might try the most understanding of owners. Arriving in England in the winter of 1825, young Binny was the sole survivor of five or six beavers shipped from Canada. William Broderip, naturalist and magistrate, took in the 'small and woolly' survivor, by then in a pitiable state, and nursed him back to health. Binny's natural environments were the gardens and garden ponds, where his taste for water lilies caused havoc. Binny however liked to straddle the best of both worlds and had access to large parts of the house – not to mention the run of the cupboards. In the interests of zoology, William Broderip watched whilst Binny collected together a range of items which, to the beaver at least, looked most promising for the construction of a 'lodge'. Dragged towards the intended location these might comprise sweeping brushes, baskets, books, boots, sticks, turf, hay, coal, cloth, and rather bizarrely, a warming pan. Piling these up in his favourite room, Binny would proceed to wall up the space between a chest of drawers and the wall, using extra turf and sticks from the garden as a roof. With remarkable forbearance, even for one of the founders of the Zoological Society, Broderip observed Binny diligently pushing and pulling 'large masses' of wooden objects through the house on his way to his construction site. In between bouts of construction,

Binny would sit with his tail in water, although it was said he was not fond of plunging his whole body into it. All of these activities were recorded by Broderip for the edification of readers of the 1830 publication *The Gardens and Menagerie of the Zoological Society Delineated*. Binny was fed mostly on a diet of bread, milk and sugar (a staple diet of many a captive animal in this period), but supplemented with succulent fruit and roots. Broderip was silent on whether Binny was allowed to collect these himself, thus creating as much chaos in the garden as there was undoubtedly in the house. Despite the undoubted trail of destruction Binny left in his wake, Broderip described the beaver as a most affectionate, and entertaining creature, with many a 'comic scene' occurring between Binny and his flat-mate, a Macauco lemur. The housekeeper and gardener probably felt otherwise.

BEE

Beehives were once commonplace in orchards and gardens, providing honey even before their essential role as pollinators was understood. Usually kept in woven bee 'skeps' they would be placed on low platforms under shelter, or in specially built niches in walls (known as bee boles). John Evelyn, the seventeenth century diarist, garden writer, and politician, had other things on his mind when he decided to keep bees. Writing in his never to be published gardening work, *Elysium Britannicum*, Evelyn noted that bees 'are of all the creatures the most affected to Monarchy, & the most Loyall, reading a Lecture of obedience to Rebells in every mans Garden.' Evelyn was a royalist and his sympathetic views of the arrangement of workers all serving the Queen in the hives owed much to his political beliefs. Others more sympathetic to the Commonwealth had argued that bees worked together for the common good, gathering, storing and harvesting. Samuel Hartlib, a zealous reformer, had published *The Reformed Commonwealth of Bees* in 1655 comparing the 'regiment of bees with the Civil Empire', Evelyn on the other hand was firmly convinced that bees needed and had 'a City, a King and an Empire'. In an age when regicide shocked the nation, the question of what happened to a bee colony if you removed the monarch was of more than usual relevance. To establish the truth, and to permit a close view of the architecture of the hive, Evelyn constructed a transparent hive that he called his 'Philosophical Apiary'. This rather gothic looking octagonal structure had a removable pointed roof with a small bust atop and was placed on a stand to allow easy viewing. Samuel Pepys (a friend of Evelyn and fellow diarist) visited the garden and hive in May 1665 and recorded 'After dinner to Mr Eveling's (*sic.*); he being abroad, we walked in his garden, and a lovely noble ground he hath indeed. And among other rarities a hive of bees hived in glass' which one could observe and contemplate this model society. John Evelyn was not the only person to envisage a glass beehive – Christopher Wren had also designed a 'pleasant and profitable' transparent hive whilst a fellow of All Souls College in the 1650s, again drawing in the fascinated Hartlib who wrote to him for details and illustration. Wren's hive was considerably less gothic than that constructed by the more flamboyant Evelyn. Careful study of the garden bees in their glass hives may not have answered the philosophical questions of the day, but at least it put paid to the notion, still prevalent in the seventeenth century, that bees spontaneously generated from the stomachs of dead cows. Bees are not the only creatures to have been compared to human social organisation. In 1864 the royal aviary at Frogmore, Windsor was stocked with birds which were reported as forming 'a constitutional monarchy, in happy and distinctive harmony', including birds representing the monarchy, the aristocracy, the peers, commons and plebeians, all 'moving together pleasantly like a well-regulated human society of the European pattern'.

BUDGERIGAR

Woburn Abbey, Bedfordshire, better known for its herds of deer, was once also home to free-flying homing budgerigars. An eccentric even by the standards of the Dukes of Bedford, the 12th Duke announced to the press in 1951 that he had managed to breed a homing budgerigar which would fly free in the daytime but come back to feed and roost. Subsequent sightings of wild budgies in the surrounding woods might indicate that this was not an entirely successful project, although much was made in the *International Herald Tribune* of the possibility of the budgerigars (a member of the parrot family) replacing homing pigeons and delivering messages orally.

BUFFALO

Travel souvenirs can take many forms, and lingering memories of foreign climes have resulted in many an exotic garden planting, out of place in the duller climes of home. Sir William Drummond Stewart perhaps had more excuse than many for his determination to bring back souvenirs to his estate in Perthshire, having spent seven years travelling in the American West. Living for part of this time with the native Americans, Sir William had found their way of life, their diet and the landscape that they lived in, greatly to his liking – so much so that on his return to Scotland he determined to bring it with him. Buffalo form a large part of the diet and culture of the West American Plains Indian, and so he determined that buffalo should also roam the grounds of his home, Murthly Castle at Rohallion. In July 1839 the *Perthshire Courier* recorded, with surprising lack of concern, the arrival of a pair of buffalo 'which passed through Perth for Murthly Castle' a fortnight ago, followed that week by four young 'Moozedeer'. Further pairs of buffalo followed as Stewart sought to establish a breeding population which would furnish him with not only fond memories of his travels, but also a constant supply of the buffalo hides which he insisted sleeping on, disposing as he had of the castle's feather bed. To allay any homesickness on the part of the buffalo, and help maintain his own illusions, Stewart also planted parts of the buffalo park with native American plants and trees. From the Rocky Mountains and the Pacific Coast came such plants, shrubs and trees as buffalo berry (*Shephardia argentea*) and bunch grass as well as tobacco root and red maples. The Douglas Fir, first introduced into the country by a fellow Scotsman in 1826, was planted in numbers around the Rohallion park, although presumably somewhat smaller specimens than the buffalo were accustomed to. These efforts to imitate the American environment in the wilds of Scotland appear to have met with approval on the part of the buffalo, as they were still roaming the grounds and terrifying guests in 1861. Not content with the live buffalo, Stewart had a pair of bizarre 'buffalo chairs' made to grace the castle hallway. Richly carved of mahogany, each took the shape of an individual buffalo complete with thickly carved curls, rosewood horns, and stout hairy forelegs. Anxious to share his love of the Americas, Stewart also sent buffalo to his friend Lord Breadalbane, at Taymouth. A herd of at least seven graced the park and were greatly admired by Queen Victoria, who described them as 'those strange hump-backed creatures from America'. Visitors to Murthly Castle who failed to be overawed by the buffalo were entertained by the sight of Sir William's two native American Indians who, when not acting as combined valet and buffalo carer, would dress up in costumes of an Indian chief to the horror of the ladies' maids, and one suspects to the equal horror of the peacefully grazing buffalos. A small stone shelter (still standing) was supposedly built for the

Indians to shelter in whilst watching the buffalo. Stewart's estate and buffalos were dispersed on his death, as his son had pre-deceased him attempting a sword-swallowing trick whilst inebriated.

BUTTERFLY

The dance of butterflies as they flit lightly between the blossoms is one of the essential elements of the English cottage garden in summer. Painted Ladies share the dance-floor with Red Admirals, whilst Peacocks strut their stuff in front of the dowdier Hedge Brown, and in their turn are outshone by the Holly Blue. Taken for granted before the arrival of pesticides, these symbols of resurrection and transformation, represent for most of us the simple joys of a carefree life. The 1970s saw a dramatic decline in their numbers, as modern chemicals extinguished not only the insects themselves, but also the numerous weed plants on which their various life stages depend. Miriam Rothschild, world famous entomologist, botanist, and member of the extended Rothschild family of wealthy bankers, was dismayed to find the family gardens at Ashton Wold bereft of these fluttering reminders of carefree joy. Agricultural intensification during the war, and later developments in mono-culture, had led to the creation of a countryside that was, in her words, reminiscent of a snooker table. Re-introducing butterflies and wild flowers to the gardens and countryside was to henceforth be one of Miriam Rothschild's passions in life, commencing with her own garden. In 1970 she created a mix of seeds to establish a traditional wild flower (and butterfly) meadow. Sown on a dilapidated tennis court, the hard, poor, soils of the court rewarded her endeavours and soon the meadow not only blossomed but, as is the way with weeds, spread. As the small stars of corncockle and daisies spangled the grass, so the butterflies returned. By the 1990s the meadow, with its nursery of caterpillars, had spread over 150 acres of the Ashton Wold gardens, invading formal gardens, springing up in old glasshouses, and poking through cracks in flagstones. The meadow garden became The butterfly garden, enveloped in a cloud of peacocks, tortoiseshells, brimstones, green-veined whites and orange tips. For Miriam Rothschild the butterflies were another dimension to the garden, like dream flowers that had broken loose from their stalks and escaped into the sunshine. In fact she referred to her butterfly garden not so much as a home for the butterflies, but a convenient hostelry where they supped on a selection of 'drinks' as in a good wayside inn or 'garden pub'. The nectar and the scent mixed with the floral fragrance exhaled by the butterflies themselves and created not only a delightful garden for humans, but also an area of sexual excitement for the butterflies. Receiving the heady mix through the chemical receptors in their tongues, antennae and feet Dame Miriam's meadows provided something rather more exotic for their inhabitants than the average wayside inn! *The Butterfly Gardener* (1983) inspired a new generation of butterfly and wildflower gardens, for whom Dame Rothschild provided her magic mix of 'Farmer's Nightmare', seeds of wildflowers for her beloved butterflies to drink from as they danced away their lives.

CAPE BARREN GOOSE

The Latin name of this goose is *Cereopsis novaehollandiae*, after the original name for its Australian native home. A large and cumbersome goose weighing up to 5kg, its numbers were predictably devastated by the early settlers. A single tame specimen graced the gardens of the Governor of New Holland in the eighteenth century and was remarked upon as 'very rare and quite splendid' with its grey plumage spotted with black, like a monochrome peacock.

CAPYBARA

Described by aficionados as a solidly built and over-large version of a guinea pig, the capybara is the largest living rodent. Partially aquatic (with webbed toes for wallowing in lake edges) and weighing in at over 100lbs, even a member of the Amateur Menagerie Club could not describe it as an ideal garden pet. That however did not stop Mr Dennis, of St Leonard's Park, Sussex, keeping twenty-eight of them in his grounds. Describing them as 'quite tame' in their natural state, Mr Dennis remarked that they had the advantage of being very tolerant of the variations of climate in this country 'disporting themselves in the open even when the thermometer has stood at freezing point and the snow has been thick on the ground'. So tolerant were they that they even produced litters of baby capybaras, comprising between three and eight babies at a time, winning Mr Dennis the 1913 Amateur Menagerie Club award for the acclimatising, breeding and rearing of any exotic animal kept at liberty. 'Liberty' in the case of St Leonard's was a forty-acre grass parkland with heather and undergrowth and a small thatched hut or shelter – bringing a hint of Africa to the Sussex coast! A lake was also added to the park to allow the capybara the chance to wallow, roll, and dive like seals. Usually slow movers, the capybara would endearingly attempt a series of small leaps in order to reach the food that was delivered daily, of hay and oats. Although Mr Dennis claimed great success with the tameness of his capybara he spoke wistfully of a friend in South America who kept them as house pets. His friend, he said, was astonished that Mr Dennis kept his out of doors as nothing could make a better indoor pet on account of their affectionate disposition and cleanly habits. The following year, Mr Dennis said, he would experiment with bringing one of his own indoors as a giant house pet. The following year instead saw the outbreak of the First World War, and put paid to an experiment that could have revolutionised the English pet industry.

CASSOWARY

At times of emotional stress a pet can be a great therapy, as evidenced by the modern introduction of 'visiting pets' into hospices and mental institutions, although these usually take the form of cats or dogs, rather than cassowaries. Rudolf II, Emperor of the Holy Roman Empire, had only recently recovered from a nervous breakdown when he was thrown into further emotional turmoil by the news that his brother had married Rudolf's own fiancé. A new therapeutic 'pet' was truly in order and fortunately for the mentally troubled Emperor, a cassowary was to hand. Although 'to hand' might seem a rather inappropriate phrase for a journey which had led this particular individual from an unknown origin (presumably its native North Australian rainforest), via a Javanese King, and a Dutch East Indian trader. Having spent eight months on the journey from its royal stopover in Java, the cassowary reached Amsterdam in July 1597, and soon attracted the attention of Count Georg Eberhard von Solms, who purchased it as a decoration for his park and pleasure ground at La Haye. Von Solms had an animal and bird collection in his extensive grounds, and the cassowary, with its strange horny helmet, long red wattles, and bright blue neck, added a certain decorative distinction to this. Solms might have been less eager had he known of its 12cm long spiky claw which can be used to deadly effect, or of its equally powerful stout legs. Holy Roman Emperors can be very persuasive and, as Rudolph II made every effort to obtain the bird, the cassowary had little time to settle into the park at La Haye before it was off on its travels again, this time to Rudolf's Royal Garden at Prague. Overjoyed with his new acquisition (and hopefully with his mind distracted from faithless siblings and unfaithful fiancées) Rudolf made arrangements for a new aviary to be constructed in the grounds especially for the New World arrival. The court painter Bartholomäus Beranek was employed to enhance the aviary with imaginative pictures of the cassowary's native tropical home, a task which one hopes was not so realistic as to cause the cassowary to rush headlong at the painted vegetation, head-butting the walls in imitation of its natural behaviour in the rainforest undergrowth. Outside of its aviary it could apparently be seen from afar, a splash of cobalt blue and raspberry red in the duller green tones of the royal garden pastures. Whether it was the cold of the

Prague winter, or the equally life threatening insistence of its collectors that it would 'eat red embers and fire', by the early 1600s the cassowary, the first ever in Europe, was listed in Rudolf's sad catalogue of dead and stuffed creatures, the Kunstkammer. For the cassowary it was the end of a long journey, and, in the circumstances, a surprisingly long life. For Rudolf it was the beginning of a search for another new pet to join his burgeoning collection in the royal gardens and to temporarily take his mind off his increasing troubles. Fortunately there were rumours of a dodo and soon yet another surprised flightless bird found itself staring past exquisite pictures of tropical lushness out into the frozen royal gardens of a Prague spring.

CAT

Serious gardeners are not known for their tolerance when it comes to cats in the flower-beds. Feline toiletry habits famously favour recently finely tilled soils, such as newly sown seed-beds and freshly weeded borders, and unpleasant surprises await the unwary gardener. Added to this the impact on a herbaceous border of a sleeping cat, particularly the plumper members of the tribe, can be devastating, and their behaviour towards plants of catmint is best passed over. All the more surprising therefore that Gertrude Jekyll, perhaps the most famous of English gardeners, adored cats and welcomed them into her gardens at Munstead Wood. Tabby, Tavy, Toozle, Tommy, Patty, Blackie, Mittens, Miss Maggie, Pinkieboy and Tittlebat were all privileged cats who dwelt with Miss Jekyll, and featured in her 1908 book *Children and Gardens*; itself a topic usually guaranteed to raise the hackles of the dedicated gardener. Tabby, a generously built cat, featured as a full-length photograph on the very first page of the book, whilst his exploits and those of his fellows were happily recounted in a chapter called 'Pussies in the Garden', a heading redolent of a more innocent age. Gertrude Jekyll was a great pioneer of garden photography, and illustrated the chapter with charming, if rather posed, pictures of Tabby in a basket, Tabby amongst the cut flowers, and Tabby in the basket of photographic plates. Rather more realistically, Tabby is also shown rolling in the *Cerastium* (a low growing plant with white daisy like flowers which, like cats, loves sunny places), and eating the catmint. Blackie we are told didn't just eat the catmint, he went berserk in it, jumping in the air on top of it, flopping down in the middle of it, dancing on it and rushing in and out of it. A silhouette drawing of Blackie in a frenzied leap is included as Miss Jekyll was, she says, not able to photograph him with the exposures available. Tittlebat on the other hand appears to have favoured dahlia destruction from an early age, aided and abetted by the genial gardener herself, who tied balls of paper and string onto the beleaguered plant to attract the feline. Each of the cats had its own favoured part of the garden, Tittlebat's sphere of influence being the Primrose Garden and the region of yew, birch and chestnut that surrounded it. Tabby frequented the nut-walk and pergola and also considered himself the warden of two gates – the hand hunting-gate through the yew hedge and the five-barred gate that crossed the back road. Not only could Miss Jekyll identify each cat by sight, she could also identify them by purr, Pinkieboy's being, we are told, 'deep in tone, not loud, but highly musical, the sound of it reminding her of the whirring wings of the Humming-bird hawk moth. To celebrate a visit by Miss Jekyll's niece, a cat tea-party was arranged, with hand-written invitations to 'Miss Jekyll, at home, 4 o'clock'. Saucers were laid with a strip of fish and cold rice pudding topped with tiny balls of butter. A formal menu card listed '*Les Filets de Hering á la Minette; Les Tranches de Riz en Traverse, Les petites bouchées de Beurre frais*', and (for desert) '*La Crème au Naturel*'. The catering was declared a great success by all, and the whole was recorded by camera for posterity. In addition to photography, Miss Jekyll also produced a series of educational sketches in *Children and Gardens*, illustrated cats in plan and elevation, neatly teaching children at whom the book is aimed, the difference between the two. Pinkie in West Elevation and Pinkie in East Elevation are two of the most delightfully quirky sketches ever to have graced a gardening book, although the plan of an 'equicateral' triangle formed by three kittens at equal distances around a milk saucer is a close third. Jekyll's cats lived with her into her magnificently eccentric old age, when they would follow their increasingly stout and imposing mistress on her slow tours of the garden, adding an air of royalty to the progression.

CHAMELEON

'Looking back I cannot imagine why I bought him, he wasn't attractively soft, beautiful to look upon, nor had he any engaging qualities'. Few pets can have made quite such a negative impression on their future owners, but the young Violet Wilson was obviously a sucker for the exotic, even if she could acknowledge that here was an excessively plain reptile. The chameleon's effect on the family would however have come as some consolation to any mischievous child, as its appearance in the drawing room caused people to stampede in all directions, hurling abuse at Violet and her pet from their vantage points of window ledges and chairs. Despite these inauspicious (if entertaining) starts, 'Billy' the chameleon inevitably found himself a home in the family's greenhouse, where it was hoped the warmth and exotic flowers would at least tempt him into performing the colour changes which the species are famous for. Alas it was the gardener rather than the chameleon that changed colour. Requested to meet the said employee downstairs, Violet discovered an 'enraged and empurpled' man. The gardener discoursed at length on the shock he had received in discovering the 'horrible creature' in his greenhouse, before handing in an ultimatum: either the chameleon went or he did. Head Gardeners were a treasured resource in the Edwardian period, and so it was Billy who found himself ousted from the greenhouse. Violet walked disconsolately around the garden with her moribund pet, musing on the soft and fluffy opossum that she had been promised for Christmas, an opossum that now seemed a distant dream following the debacles in the drawing room and greenhouse. Suddenly Billy livened up and, darting out his long tongue, caught a fly on the wing. This manoeuvre had the unlikely effect of endearing him at once to Violet's sister, herself a lover of exotic animals. A shrewd showman, Violet's sister could also spot an opportunity for a little extra pocket money. From then on Billy's celebrity career was assured, as visitors to the family home were pressed into accompanying the chameleon and his new owner around the garden demonstrating his taste for bluebottles. Shrieks of mingled joy and terror could be heard as the normally immobile reptile dispatched yet another irritating and disease spreading fly. The celebrity success of Billy's 'garden tours' might be seen as an testimony to either the lack of entertainment possibilities in the Edwardian period, or the dire need for fly controls in the days before refrigerators. A crisp photograph of Billy survives demonstrating clearly his unusually immobile qualities in an age before rapid-aperture photography.

CHAMELEON II

The Victorian naturalist and author, Reverend Theodore Wood, also kept a chameleon which he would often take into the garden for exercise and to watch its 'strange habits'. The strange habits in this instance did not include horrifying or entertaining visitors with fly catching, but took the rather plainer form of walking. This alone was enough to entertain the Reverend who described the garden jaunts in his 1890 work *Petland Revisited*. 'The reptile', he said, 'could get over the ground at a tolerable pace; that is to say, it would win a race against a tortoise. Its mode of progression can scarcely be named; it was not walking, nor running, nor sprawling, nor waddling, but a unique mixture of them all. It bore about the same relation to the walk of ordinary animals as does the hobble of a man with two wooden legs to the stately march of the drum-major in the Guards'. In case anyone wanted to imitate a chameleon taking its daily constitutional he also gave hints on how a person might achieve the same stance. Let any person who wishes to walk like a chameleon 'stoop and rest upon his hands and the tips of his toes, taking care to spread the hands and to hold them with the thumbs pointing directly backwards and the fingers forwards, as to get his elbows well out'. A tail, made of a trailing wooden rod should be affixed to the waistcoat and then 'let him try and run the stipulated distance within a given time' over a path strewn with brushwood and large flints. The result would, according to Rev. Wood, be a passing imitation of a chameleon walking up a garden path. Whether through trying to admire the chameleon or the Reverend, the neighbours must have spent much time peering over the garden fence!

COATI

Also known as the Brazilian Weasel, or the Coati-Mondi (*Nasua narica*), this small raccoon-like animal, with its tendency to tear the heads off chickens, steal eggs, and turn pickpocket, may seem less than an ideal inhabitant for the country cottage garden. However nothing seems to daunt a prospective pet owner and it comes as no surprise that a coati called 'Kiko' enjoyed the run of a garden owned by a Victorian sea captain and his family of six children. What is surprising, given the record of his activities, is that the family went on to describe him as 'the most affectionate and amusing pet' they ever had, leaving one to speculate wildly on the antics and characters of their other animal companions. Kiko originally made his home in the house, but obviously bored with the possibilities this held for mischief, soon graduated to the garden. Here he commenced by helpfully grubbing up snails before demonstrating the use of his very strong and flexible snout in searching for worms amongst the bedding plants. Furrowing through bedding displays is an established way in which to make an enemy of any gardener and Tim, the gardener at this establishment, was no exception. Seeing Kiko commence his random cultivations, Tim would attempt to pelt him with anything to hand. At this the nimble creature would retaliate by running up one of the poplar trees in the garden and pelting the gardener in return with twigs broken off the tree, thus adding arboricultural injury to horticultural insult. Whilst engaged in this mutual exchange of weaponry the coati would call out 'kiko-kiko', from which he derived his name. The author of *Petland Revisited*, in which book this wonderful history appears, did not see fit to record what the gardener called out in reply. Vantage points held a great fascination for Kiko, and as well as the trees he would climb onto the top of the garden wall, unexpectedly leaping down onto passers by, and clinging around their necks. It was the garden wall that became his downfall, as he took to dismantling it stone by stone, picking out all the mortar and throwing down the stones. Despite his other endearing habits of egg stealing, terrifying visitors, and stealing the neighbours' Sunday dinner, he was eventually given away in an attempt to save the garden walls from complete destruction, not to mention the loss of a good gardener. His new home was apparently also short-lived as he added climbing inside women's petticoats to his list of hobbies. In the puritan atmosphere of Victorian Wales, this was further evidence that in the words of the Captain's neighbours, the little coati was 'the devil' in disguise.

COW

John Claudius Loudon, Victorian garden designer, promoter of public parks, commentator on cemeteries, campaigner for education, and all round workaholic, divided gardens into four classes or rates. In his 1838 (752 page!) work *The Suburban Gardener and Villa Companion*, Loudon advised that the difference between a second-rate garden and a third-rate garden was that the second-rate would have alongside its garden a paddock and small dairy. A cow, he claimed, being to a person with a family, one of the principal sources of comfort derivable from a country residence, which perhaps does not say much for his view of family life. Anxious that both country and urban cows were generally being kept in unhealthy conditions, Loudon specified that cows that graced second-rate gardens should be provided with a cowhouse of ample size, with complete drainage and thorough ventilation; all set within an attractive grassed paddock. The paddock should be 'harmonised with the pleasure ground of the property, and rendered ornamental by scattering a few trees over it ... and by the judicious disposal and planting of the drinking pond'. Suitable trees listed by Loudon included acers, robinia, mesphilus, and poplars, as well as apple, pear, cherry and plum. Fortunately for the trees, and their purchasers, Loudon also thoughtfully included several designs for protection against the predations of 'horned cattle'. Anxious that the cow should not be lonely in her spacious and well appointed paddock and decorative cow-shed, Loudon further recommended that a pet goat, lamb or donkey should be purchased to form a 'companionable attachment' for the bovine. Regardless of her social life, the cow would also need to be combed and brushed every day, in the manner of a horse, and fresh straw or leaves be used in the shed to provide a soft and 'elastic' bed. To induce the pampered cow to take exercise and keep in good health Loudon suggested that the paddock and planting be so designed as to have the end of it concealed. Thus, one supposes, drawing the cow on to admire the hidden views and appreciate the artistry of the landscape designer. George Stacey Gibson of Saffron Walden (Essex) was the proud owner of a copy of

Loudon's *The Suburban Gardener and Villa Companion*, and an equally proud owner of just such a second-rate garden as Loudon had in mind. Hill House, bought by Gibson in 1845, was designed in almost exact imitation of the second-rate gardens extolled in Loudon's work. The gardens contained pleasure grounds, a formal garden, lawns, conservatory, rose garden, kitchen garden and that all-important promoter of family felicity, a cow paddock complete with cow. For the greater comfort of the cow, a substantial cowshed was constructed, and a meandering path led through a mixed tree and shrub border around the edges of the paddock. Located next to the main pleasure grounds and lawn the cow (and paddock) made an aesthetically pleasing adjunct to the gardens of Hill House, as well of course, as establishing without doubt that the gardens were second, rather than merely third, rate. When the gardens were eventually sold in 1934, a Jersey cow was sold with them.

COW II

In 1873 the Cotterall Dormer family also decided to enhance their parkland at Rousham (Oxfordshire) with attractive bovine decoration. They chose the aesthetically pleasing shorthorns, Faustina Gwynne and her sister Goody Gwynne. Brilliant chestnut with white speckles, the sisters were to prove as feisty as they were attractive. Escaping their idyllic home, originally designed by William Kent, they took to village visiting and would chase the local people down the small high street. Nothing could turn the Cottrell Dormers against the sisters however, and the family even commissioned a painting of Faustina, who appears as a large, flat backed, but undeniably attractive creature. When Faustina eventually died at the age of twenty-two a stone slab was erected in her memory. Her sister Goody does not appear to have been honoured in the same way and may justifiably have complained of discrimination. Rousham still boasts a fine herd of cattle, but they are the rare white long-horns, and appear considerably less adventurous if just as aesthetically pleasing.

CROCODILE

Lengths of rusting piping and old hot water tanks are relatively common features on neglected garden sites, whether they be remnants of grand conservatories or old allotments. The tanks in the Victorian gardens at Eller How (Cumbria) were however far from usual. A small country house, Eller How had been built in 1851, and in 1863 was purchased by the rather eccentric garden lover and inventor, Henry Boyle. Henry and his wife Nellie lived a financially precarious life, with Henry continually expending money on expanding the gardens, and then having to re-mortgage the property. A recluse from village society, Henry spent his days constructing grottoes, sunken glasshouses, a massive stone tower, and underground tunnels, and of course the mysterious water tanks. The sunken glasshouses may be explained by his passion for fern collecting and the creation of covered rockeries to provide the fern's favourite conditions. Coloured glass was used to create the right light for tree ferns whilst moisture encouraged *Todea* and other 'Filmy Ferns'. Through his correspondence with Kew Botanic Gardens there is plentiful evidence also for Henry's collection of water lilies and other aquatics, including the giant Amazonian water lily (*Victoria amazonica*). In fact Henry's brother claimed that Henry had been the second person ever to manage to flower this giant in the open air. However, the massive warm water tanks and underground tunnels which Henry had hewn into the rock of the Lake District held more than just lilies. His neighbours, the Mackereth family (whose grandfather had once owned the land on which Henry's garden was built) recalled being taken as young children to see Henry's gardens. Held over the wall, they had looked down to see his collection of crocodiles swimming in the ferneries below. At least two young crocodiles were said to be kept by Henry until they 'grew too big even for his liking'. When these reptiles might have arrived is not known. Certainly not when the house was being 'let out' in yet another attempt by Henry to recoup his financial outlays on the gardens, but perhaps when Henry and Nellie lived there in the 1870s. These years also saw Henry filing a patent for an incubator

for keeping eggs at a constant temperature and such a device would also be invaluable for keeping two crocodiles at their favourite temperature. Alas he seems either to have neglected to use the thermostats himself, or perhaps neglected to instruct his staff on how to do so, as local legend has it that one night the gardener left the boiler heat on all night and the unfortunate crocodiles were literally boiled alive. An unfortunate accident for a family called 'Boyle' and one that seemed to cast an air of myth upon the reptilian story. All that remained of the gardens at Eller How after the family finally left it were the extensive subterranean tunnels, hand dug by the reclusive Henry, the complex of tanks and steps and a rustic tower. In 2000 a garden restoration project re-excavated the fernery and the tunnels, and put water lilies back in the tanks. Striving for that extra piece of authenticity they also introduced a young (male) alligator called Alice to the site. As Alice swam happily amongst the aquatic tanks before slithering of to explore the darkness of the tunnels beyond, it suddenly all seemed very believable!

CROCODILE II

James I, that monarch of unfinished schemes, had a plan to keep crocodiles in the then un-drained parts of St James's park. Fortunately for the populace, the marshes proved too cold. James was instead forced to restrict himself to cows and waterfowl.

CROW

Whether the result of the hunter's instincts of the Wild West, or the still alarming proximity of the natural world red in tooth and claw, tales of unusual pets do not litter the history of American gardens in the same way that they do English. However Cudjo the crow was one of several whose stories appear in Olive Thorne Miller's 1882 book *Queer Pets and Their Doings*. Recounting the 'true and authenticated' tales of a family living on the edge of a pleasant village near New York, all the usual dogs, cats, and bears appear in their turn in the garden. Cudjo the crow however strikes a note of novelty. Rescued when the cotton-tree that housed his nest was felled, Cudjo was the sole survivor of the nestlings. Successfully brought up on a diet of egg and meats, he was allowed free range of the house and gardens, always returning at feeding time, which he shared with the house dog. His weakness appears to have been hats, as he would sit on a tree and swoop down on tradesmen, neighbouring gardeners, and even the organ-grinder's monkey, to liberate headwear and add it to his own collection. In imitation of the magpie's habit of collection, Cudjo was also attracted to shiny objects including coins, thimbles, and small items of cutlery. Eventually these missing objects were tracked to a series of mounds under the piazza in the garden. Being opened, in the nature of an archaeological investigation, this was found to contain a six-bladed knife, a rosary (apparently blessed by the bishop and originally belonging to a servant), some copper cents, a glass eye from a stuffed owl, a small china dog, bits of glass, a gold ring and 'a few silver spoons'. Fish also attracted his avarice (or maybe his appetite) and during the five years of his life the garden pond was emptied of its stock, which was secreted around the garden as dead bodies. Similarly unfortunate were the rabbits and chickens who shared the garden with the crow, and whose babies were regularly subjected to attacks. An appetite for wet cement apparently spelt the end for what appears to have been one of the least attractive of the garden pets described in this book!

DEMOISELLE CRANE

Versailles, that vast and splendid monument to the power of Louis XIV, contained within its gardens all manner of exotic plants, animals and birdlife. The brilliantly plumaged courtiers that surrounded Louis whiled away their days in outdoor theatre, sailing along the Grand Canal in the park, and visiting the menageries and aviaries of pelicans, ostriches and cassowaries. Most popular of the many birds that inhabited the gardens were the Demoiselle Cranes, a smaller more delicately built species than the common crane, and with a more balletic dancing display than their larger cousins. This dance, with its graceful and skilful jumps, bows and curtseys, and the cranes elegant gait, led to their being compared to the gypsy dancers, (or *bohemiennes*) whose dance they were said to imitate. To prevent stocks of such a decorative bird becoming low, a special animal purveyor was sent under orders from Louis' Chief Minister to obtain the cranes from their home grounds of Africa, along with ostriches, guinea fowl and purple swamphens. Once at Versailles the birds, of whom six arrived, were said to crave the attention of their court admirers, following people around not for the titbits of food that might be thrown, but instead to attract an audience for their 'dancing and singing'. A case of courting the courtier! Even the rather less flirtatiously minded fellows of the *Académie Royale des Sciences* were sufficiently charmed by the Demoiselle to record and describe their dances in their *Mémoires pour servir à l'histoire naturelle des animaux;* a work which otherwise concentrated almost exclusively on the anatomy of fifty different exotic animals. Charming the *Académie*, whose usual occupation consisted of systematic dissection, was surely a testimony to the bohemian lure of the demoiselle dance. English visitors were also entranced, describing the cranes as having a graceful symmetry of form and tasteful disposition of plumage, gentle and good tempered. In the catalogue of animals and birds in the gardens of Versailles the Demoiselle Cranes were catalogued as '*bateleur*', the French for tumbler, acrobat or magician, a testimony to their skilled footwork. Louis XV was later to replace their graceful charms with the wilder pleasures of the lion, leopard and tiger, whilst paintings within the palace itself depicted hunting scenes of crocodile and ostrich to the taste of this bloodthirsty ruler, for whom the dancers held lesser charms. A pictorial record of the animal and bird inhabitants of the Versailles botanic gardens by Jean-Baptist Oudry testify to the lingering presence of the Demoiselles, joined by their cousins the Crowned Cranes, frozen by the painter in mid-dance. When the mob arrived to 'share their liberty' with the birds and animals at Versailles any surviving cranes would have been loosed into the adjoining forests and woodland, where as late as 1840 the Inspector of Forests noted an unlikely assortment of exotics living and breeding, and, one likes to think, dancing.

DINGO

The seaside walks and esplanades of fashionable Victorian Brighton provided gentle exercise for those in search of rest or recuperation. Fashionable families, hopeful spinsters and invalid children promenaded past the Royal Pavilion, admiring the exoticism of its architecture and the exquisiteness of its gardens. In 1885 promenaders would have the opportunity of experiencing the exotic in the rather more lively form of Walter Rothschild's tame dingo. The dingo was accompanying the seventeen year old on a six-week long convalescence from a 'tiresome cough'. Staying at the Princes Hotel, she accompanied her owner on his walks, being led on a collar and chain and attracting, unsurprisingly, universal attention. Her liveliness and 'unreliability' was apparently very troublesome, although it is unclear from Walter's biography whether the trouble was caused to Walter or the hotel staff. Perhaps it was romantic or maternal separation that caused such trouble on the esplanades, as the previous year the dingo had been successfully mated with another pet dingo, and produced a litter of eight. Her temper in the first weeks of maternity had also been fractious, and she had ravaged the stables attacking several horses. Rather more reliable was the Australian opossum that Walter had also brought with him to Brighton. The opossum spent every day asleep under Walter's writing-desk, emerging as if by clockwork every evening at nightfall to run amok in the hotel bedrooms. Walter and his dingo would not, one feels, have taken kindly to the 'no dogs' regulations in force on Brighton's beaches nowadays.

DINOSAUR

Unsurprisingly, live dinosaurs have not been a common garden pet, but the Dinosaur Court at Crystal Palace gardens come as close as one can get to encountering this animal amongst the flowerbeds. When the park was first laid out in the 1850s, the study of dinosaurs was still at a rudimentary stage. The very word had only been coined in 1842, but enthusiasm for these newly discovered creatures was running high and a dinosaur park was a 'must have' for the Victorian park designers. In 1853 the park directors asked the dinosaur expert Professor Richard Owen to design a series of life size creatures to thrill and educate the Victorian public. The models were to be made of stone and concrete and were actually modelled by Benjamin Waterhouse Hawkins under the directions of Richard Owen. In 1854 Hawkins gave a talk on the difficulties encountered in reconstructing dinosaur species about which little was known, and giving a vivid insight into the problems of casting models which used 640 bushels of artificial stone and endless stucco. Each of the dinosaurs (including *Ichthyosaurus* and *Plesiosaurus* which are apparently not technically dinosaurs) were placed in replica environments in which they would be at home. 'Tidal' waters rose and fell with the demand from the surrounding fountains, giving the impression that the dinosaurs were dragging themselves out of the water. Hawkins' helpful inclusion of the names of the various strata written on the rock outcrops on which the dinosaurs were placed must have added a touch of unreality; the *Megalosaurus* for example stalked determinedly away from an outcrop labelled with the words 'Oolite'. Model plants which the prehistoric giants might have eaten were also included, although in the case of the giant carnivorous

Megalosaurus, the smaller dinosaurs were quite enough of a snack. To celebrate the completion of the dinosaurs a grand New Years Eve banquet was served inside the *Iguanodon* at Crystal Palace Park. In fact, technically, it was served inside the cast or mould, as this was marginally bigger than the final 'statue', and could fit all the guests. Twenty-one people were served, with Professor Richard Owen (literally) at the head of the table. The names of famous dinosaur 'hunters' including Buckland and Cuvier were displayed on the pink and white striped tent that covered the entire ensemble. The dinosaurs cost a hefty £13,700, and although a small income was made by selling replica small-scale models at £30 a group, some remained unfinished. The Crystal Palace Park was extremely popular and the models there provided the popular vision of dinosaurs long after research gave new insights, proving for example that the long nose 'horn' on one should actually have been placed as a claw on its 'thumb'! Long overdue restoration in 2001 returned many of these giant monsters and their prehistoric surroundings to their former glory, but the *Anaplotherium* (a sort of giant hippopotamus) has unfortunately gone missing; nearby residents are advised to check their garden sheds.

DOG

Small gardens and large dogs are not often thought an ideal combination, but when the celebrated poet, critic and garden creator, Alexander Pope, moved to his Twickenham Villa in 1719 he brought with him his elderly mother, his childhood nurse and his Great Dane, Bounce. Working with the garden designer William Kent, Pope proceeded to tunnel under the adjoining road to enlarge his garden, creating an underground grotto, and linking the house to the Thames. Whilst Kent designed temples and Pope laid out serpentine walks in the villa garden, Bounce carved out her own career amongst the celebrities of the day. Bounce appears in sketches of the gardens at Twickenham by William Kent as he designed ever more unlikely looking shell temples. Bounce is also portrayed in Richardson's portrait of Pope gazing fondly up at her master. A gift from the Prince of Wales of minerals for the underground grotto was reciprocated by a present of one of Bounce's next litter of puppies. Sent to the Prince at Kew, it's collar was engraved with a rhyming couplet by Pope 'I am His Highness' Dog at Kew; Pray tell me Sir, whose Dog are you?' Other offspring soon graced some of the most famous gardens of the eighteenth century. Lord Burlington at Chiswick, Lord Harley at Wimpole, Lord Cobham at Stowe and Lord Bathurst at Cirencester all had Bounce's offspring literally bounding across their newly created English landscape parks. Whilst others 'who Arms or Arts adorned' awaited infants yet unborn, although none but Peers of 'wit and grace, can hope a puppy of [her] race'. Following in her master's footsteps Bounce herself found time to dash off an 'Heroick Epistle' from 'a Dog at Twickenham to a Dog at Court' decrying the fashion for foppishness and fawning amongst the lapdogs of the court.

> FOP! you can dance, and make a Leg,
> Can fetch and carry, cringe and beg,
> And (what's the Top of all your Tricks)
> Can stoop to pick up Strings and Sticks.
> We Country Dogs love nobler Sport,
> And scorn the Pranks of Dogs at Court.

Bounce's final resting place is unknown, although it is rumoured that there was more than one Bounce and thus more than one resting place. However one of her offspring was buried in the grotto at Prior Park, and is now the 'property' of the National Trust. A fitting end to one of the most famous dogs in garden history.

DOG II

An eccentric recluse, the famous nineteenth century garden writer, William Robinson, might have been expected to keep exotic animals at his garden at Gravetye Manor, Sussex. As ever, he defied expectations and kept instead a small fox terrier called Boy. Boy was an identical match to Edward VII's favourite dog, and the famous 'His Master's Voice' mascot. A stone kennel, in keeping with the stone medieval manor house of Gravetye, was built especially for Boy in the corner of the front courtyard. For most of the day the terrier accompanied Robinson around the gardens, relieving the old man's loneliness. Robinson's favourite and much exhibited flowers were his Tufted Pansies, and rounding the corner with a visitor one day, Robinson, renowned for his short temper, discovered Boy lying on a favourite patch of these delicate plants. Expecting an outburst, the visitor was astonished when instead Robinson merely uttered 'Oh, Boy', in his most reproachful voice. The reproach was sufficient and the dog sheepishly got up and returned to the garden path.

DOG III

That great writer and gardener Vita Sackville-West, also kept dogs, first at Knole, then abroad, and finally at her house and gardens at Sissinghurst, Kent. Her Alsatian, Martha, is included in perhaps the best known of all Sissinghurst photographs, posing next to Vita on the stone steps leading down to the garden. The picture hides a tragedy as Martha, then thirteen, was already dying from an incurable illness and a few weeks later Vita wrote to Harold Nicolson to tell of the 'ultimate betrayal' as Martha was put to sleep. Before Martha there had been Rollo, an Alsatian dog so sensitive that 'he seemed to read your thoughts': intelligent, handsome, but with a tendency to aggression towards visitors, the perfect match for Vita. In comparison the saluki or gazelle-hound which Vita had been given by the explorer Gertrude Bell in Baghdad had been spiritless, and after moving to Persia she had taken care to give it to a Persian prince, who lost it in a Moscow park. So enamoured was Vita Sackville-West by dogs that her final book, written in 1961, was *Faces: Profiles of Dogs* an unlikely departure from her novels, poetry and gardening columns.

DONKEY

Donkeys were once widely used in gardens to pull small carts and lawn mowers. Gertrude Jekyll, that most famous of women gardeners, had the assistance of a donkey called Jack. Miss Jekyll was most enamoured of Jack, calling him her 'handsome donkey' and providing him with a donkey shed in one part of the garden. Jack formed one of the subjects of her experiments in amateur photography, and a picture survives of him waiting outside the door to her studio with a cartload of logs for the ingle fire. When Jack died after many years of faithful service, he was rumoured to be buried in one of the giant 12ft pits that Jekyll continually dug to bury garden rubbish and to manure the poor sandy soils of Munstead Wood. Usually the resting place of more modestly sized dead rabbits, these pits were then planted over with the giant lily, *Lilium giganteum* (now *Cardiocrinum*). Thus, the apocryphal tale has it, Jack became a permanent resident in one of the world's most famous gardens, his resting spot marked by an extra large giant lily. In Jekyll's own words 'Death is the Giver of the greater new Life', 'a never ending parable of Life and Death and Immortality'.

DORMOUSE

Much cherished by the Romans, edible dormice (*Glis glis*) were kept in specially constructed pots in Roman villa gardens. These large terracotta pots (*dolia*) had breathing holes for the dormouse and an interior spiral ledge for sleeping and exercising. Nuts and other edibles would be inserted through the heavy terracotta lids that prevented the mice escaping. Ceramic pots were an essential, as the diet of the dormouse includes wood; however they also looked more attractive in the garden. Three such pots were found in the gardens of Pompeii when the site was excavated from under the cloud of ash that famously engulfed it. Many centuries later Lord Rothschild introduced edible dormice into his animal collection at Tring, from which they escaped and spread. Despite presumably slow progress, they can now be found in many gardens around Aylesbury and Luton.

DOVE

The Romans were also the first to record keeping doves in their gardens, and the Roman garden author Varro recommended his readers to paint their dovehouses white. If you were bent on attracting more doves you could also perfume the dovehouse with frankincense and sage, sprinkle their foods with wine, and their feathers with myrrh. The sweetness of your own doves' breath would apparently then attract your neighbours doves, intent on sharing in the feast. Given the cost of frankincense and myrrh it might have been cheaper to just raise your own! Kentwell Hall, Long Melford, Suffolk has had a dovehouse (or in Suffolk dialect, a 'duffus') for centuries. An early version is shown on a map of 1613, but even before that records show that doves were being kept for their eggs, meat and manure. Enriching a garden with dove manure may seem a time-consuming vision to the owner of a single dove, but the owners of Kentwell boasted 576 nesting boxes, giving a total of over 1,100 adult doves, not to mention the 'squabs' or babies. Although perhaps taking the doves beyond the pet category (few could recall the names and appearance of a thousand individual doves!) it certainly gives them a more prominent role in the garden. Dovehouses were a status symbol in the medieval and early modern period, with licences for the keeping of doves only being granted to the lords of the manor. Thus they beautified the garden, fed the house and advertised the status of their owner. Feeding a thousand or more birds (and some dovehouses could hold over 4,000 birds) might be thought to be an expensive hobby. However, the beauty of the dove is in its flight, which usually carries it well beyond the boundaries of the garden into the corn fields of your neighbours. Feeding on seeds and green shoots the doves thus terrorised the surrounding farmers, feeding on your neighbours hard work and rewarding you with the produce. The squabs raised in the nesting boxes, up to six squabs per brood, and three broods a year, would be collected and eaten as a delicacy. Collection was by means of a central ladder (known as a potence) that could be rotated around the walls of the dovehouse where the nesting boxes were built. The Kentwell dovehouse now holds the ornamental breed of fantail whites, although a tendency to become overly familiar with the wild pigeons often produces a clutch of brown and grey speckled youngsters. Still occasionally eaten during Kentwell's Tudor re-creation week, the dove has a strong, gamey taste rather at odds with its pure white plumage and soft cooing call.

DUCK

Ducks are the traditional inhabitants of many a garden, compensating the garden owner with their pale bluish-white eggs in exchange for trampled flowers and devastated wildlife. Humphry (sic.), a handsome Indian runner drake could give no such recompense for any such trespass, but instead won his owners heart with his affectionate ways. Born in the early years of the twentieth century, Humphry was given as a six-week old duck to Muriel Kenny, who kept him in her garden. Deprived of society of his own kind, Humphry, in the words of his owner, developed a passion for human society. Garden visitors were escorted round by this companionable duck, who would maintain a low conversational twitter along the route, pausing only to snack on any snails which his previous patrols had overlooked. The duties of the gardener were similarly shadowed, with Humphry spending many an hour solemnly pacing behind the roller or the mowing machine, a devoted companion in all the gardening tasks. When accompanying his mistress on her garden perambulations Humphry would go so far as to hold her skirt in his beak, ensuring that they walked side by side. Especial family friends were greeted with the bobbing and quacking usually reserved for female ducks, whilst returns from holiday or other absences were marked by extravagant displays of little jumps in imitation of the demoiselle cranes. Despite his part-time role of garden guide, Humphry still managed to fit in all the duties expected of a (male) duck, disposing of as many as thirty large snails at a single meal, including the shells. Alas his choice of vegetable foods was less exemplary and it was to the best treasures of the garden that he turned for the accompaniment to his main course. No punishment was ever discovered that made the slightest impression on him, and the culprit was forgiven much, for he repeatedly transgressed the limitations of a garden pet, being found unexpectedly in drawing rooms, or part way up the stairs. Alas for Humphry, he felt the garden was not large enough a domain, and he started to spend time hanging out by the garden gate, anxious not only to widen his circle of acquaintances, but also to expand his horizons. Opportunities soon came his way and he became a travelling duck, promenading frequently to a pool about half a mile away, often accompanied by an admiring friend. A duck should choose his walking companions carefully, and some of these may well have been wolves in sheep's clothing, as one day Humphry disappeared never to be seen again.

DUCK II

In May 2007 the Courtyard Gardens at Cambridge University Library became host to a nesting mallard, undoubtedly on the run from the plethora of tourists punting on the River Cam. Taking up residence in the raised courtyard beds she successfully laid and hatched ten eggs. A flurry of activity amongst Library staff and academic readers led to the hasty purchase of a small children's paddling pool, supplemented, as the ducklings grew, by a larger pool. The courtyard was closed to readers, and sandwiches, teas and respite from studies, had to be taken elsewhere. By the end of August, six ducklings remained, with their hard-pressed mother who had fought off passing magpies to bring up her brood. Supplementary feeding (and pool cleaning) by a dedicated member of staff meant that all were healthy and happy, in fact perhaps rather too healthy and happy, as they showed no signs of leaving. Concerns that the tall buildings surrounding the courtyard were perhaps forming a barrier to take-off were quashed by the increasingly frequent absences of the mother, presumably to ascertain whether the frenetic punting activities had lessened at all. Throughout the summer, posters and newsletters of the progress of the hatchlings had been posted on the entrance to the closed courtyard garden, and library users had taken a lively interest. Recognising the hopefully temporary nature of the residency, it was decided to maintain a suitably academic 'distance', avoiding for instance naming competitions or 'hug a duck' days. Despite this reluctance it was inevitable that a name would be found at least for the mother. Given the readership of the library one might have thought of a classical name, perhaps Semiramis, the Assyrian queen, Cleopatra, or at least Lady Clare, the founder of one of the colleges. Instead the rather intellectual mallard became Mrs Duck! At the age of ten weeks, after cutting of supplementary rations had led them to take on the role of unpaid under-gardeners in light pruning, weed and pest control, the ducklings started to explore the nearby rooftops and the final flight to liberty was expected as I write. It is hoped that next summer will see a return of the studious ducks to entertain those human academics left behind by their own species in the summer holiday migrations.

ELEPHANT

A moonlit night in Paris, the strains of the *Conservatoire de Musique*, a private 'box', what could be more natural than that a young couple should fall in love? At least that was the plan of the audience at the *Jardin des Plantes* in post-Revolutionary France. The young couple in question were Hans and Marguerite, young elephants from Ceylon, who had arrived in France from Holland, along with their English keeper. Originally Hans and Parki, (as she was then known) they had been residents at the grand gardens and palace of Het Loo, where they had been kept as pets, allowed to roam the formal gardens and grounds, and even, it was said, to enter the palace where they were plied with titbits and wine by the aristocrats at the court of William V. After a year of playing havoc with the topiary, they were moved to the menagerie at Het Groote Loo, a journey undertaken by canal barge. On the invasion of Holland by the French, the elephants were threatened with death until their safety was secured on the pleas of their keeper, Thompson. Instead of death they faced a further emigration, this time to revolutionary France. Housed in their own Eden, at the *Jardin des Plantes*, the elephants were accorded every hospitality that the newly liberated France could afford them. In return they exhibited a range of emotions complementary to their admirers; being open and friendly creatures, wise and cautious, faithful and prudent ... perhaps having something to teach the revolutionary population in this respect. In one emotion only did they fail the Parisian populace; they were 'too shy' to make love. Although clearly 'deeply devoted' to each other Hans and Marguerite were thought to have been too young to have mated on their arrival in Paris, and too shy subsequently. Their enclosure giving little of the romance of their home country, their 'primitive instincts' had lain dormant since their arrival in France. To overcome their bashfulness and re-awaken their '*sentiment d'amour*', two concerts of music were planned. These, it was hoped, would result in the couple being carried away with emotion sufficient to fulfil the expectations of their anxious audience. In true Gallic style, titbits of food were arrayed to tempt the loving couple, whilst concert musicians played operatic arias, string trios and a Haydn symphony, the musicians being placed discretely out of sight. The presence of a large audience egging on their amours was slightly more unusual but did not seem to unduly undermine the sentiments of the evening. Hans and Marguerite moved 'in measure' uttered strange cries, twined themselves around each other and flapped their ears. Their trunks moved more skilfully than '*les mains lascives*' and Marguerite was soon seen to be '*en proie à sa passion*' with every movement described by their audience as 'moving inexorably towards fulfilment'. Consummation (at least for the elephants) was however not achieved, and despite a second concert some days later the naturalist Houel was still unable to confirm his proposition that this, the most anthropomorphised of animals, made love face to face. Although this did not prevent him drawing such an event. For Hans and Marguerite, the *Jardin des Plantes* was indeed a Garden of Eden, but one with rather too many spectators for them to taste of the fruits of love.

ELEPHANT II

At the beginning of the ninth century, the Holy Roman Emperor Charlemagne sent an edict out to all countries in his Empire, instructing them in administrative, legal and agricultural matters. Being a garden lover, Charlemagne included in his edict what should be in the gardens of 'every man' throughout his empire. Included in his list were flowers including roses, and herbs such as fennel, lovage and rosemary. Strangely absent, however, was an elephant house. Charlemagne himself kept an elephant in his gardens in Aachen for over ten years. As with so many exotic animals, this eighth century traveller had been a gift from one great ruler to another. The Abbasid Caliph of Baghdad, Harun al-Rashid, sent the elephant following an ambassadorial visit to Baghdad on behalf of the Frankish Emperor. In fact the elephant was a distinctly 'second hand' offering, having been originally given to Caliph Al-Mahdi, (Harun's predecessor) by an Indian raja. Named Abu l'-Abbas, the elephant set out on his long journey from Baghdad to Charlemagne's palace and gardens in 797. Travelling by boat to Pisa, and then along the old Via Cassia from Rome to Turin, the well-travelled pachyderm had to pass over the Alps before finally arriving at Charlemagne's court at Aachen. Some sources claim it took the elephant several years to make this momentous journey, and one wonders how its keepers managed for food and shelter along the way. The embassy was accompanied by the governor of Egypt, Ibrahim Ibn al-Aghlab, who must have been more than a little relieved to arrive with the Caliph's gift still alive. On arrival at the Frankish court a special elephant house was created in the gardens of the palace. Abu l'-Abbass lived happily in this well-deserved garden retreat for almost a decade before his travelling days started again. When King Godfred of the Danes seized traders from Lübeck, taking them to Hedeby near Schleswig in Northern Germany, Charlemagne decided that he would march to Schleswig, taking Abu l'-Abbas with him to impress and quell the Danes. Unfortunately the elephant died at Lippenham on Luneburg Heath, perhaps worn out by his travels and despairing of ever seeing his warm garden-house again. Abu incidentally means 'father of', although there is no word of his descendants.

EMU

Philanthropist, tea merchant, astronomer, saviour of Wimbledon Common and Burnham Beeches, and owner of the entire parish and village of Rousden, Sir Henry Peek (MP) might be thought a little short of time for omelette making; but his were no normal omelettes. In 1891, the port of Axmouth had seen the arrival of three emus destined to embellish Sir Henry's elaborate gardens and shrubberies. Arriving 'with dignity' the emus had been forced to alight from their travelling cart and loaded into crates for the onward journey to Rousden. Four men carried the crates on their shoulders, finally arriving with their load at 1.30am. They were all said to be 'exhausted' by the journey, although it is not certain whether the report meant the men or the emus. The emus must have recovered from their trials, as several years later Sir Henry's son, Cuthbert (himself a collector of all things eclectic and exotic) was able to proffer an emu egg to a luncheon club menu held at the Camera Club in Bridport. The dinner was comprised of kangaroo tail and saddle of rein-deer, followed by the astounding 2lb emu egg. The egg was delivered to the diners and its contents removed 'on the spot' before being cooked into an omelette of 'fascinating delicacy' the size of a soup plate. Cuthbert Peek claimed that the emu that had laid the egg was some fifty years old, and that it had laid many others, some of which had been similarly prepared for the adventurous Victorian gourmet. Perhaps the delicate taste was in part due to the almost free range life led by the emus at Rousden, where they joined other curious wildfowl and 'splendid beasts' from Spain, India, South America and Africa – all allowed to wander loose in the grounds. Although a special house was constructed for the birds, they often joined the giraffe that wandered amongst the herbaceous borders. One guest recorded its attempts to 'open up friendly relationships with strangers', perplexing for the weekend visitor who had not expected to make polite conversation with a giraffe. Not all encounters were so friendly, or guests so discriminating between garden decorations and game birds. One drunken guest shot an emu under the impression that it was a large pheasant, which says little for the standard of game parties held by the Peeks. Its partner was said to have pined away from the unfortunate loss.

EMU II

It would be difficult for most tourists to decide on a specific highlight of their visit to the baroque palace and vast and magnificent grounds of Blenheim. For the naturalist Frank Buckland however the choice was easy. 'No part', he wrote in his 1875 *Log Book of a Fisherman and Zoologist*, 'of this beautiful domain can be of greater interest to the true lover of animal history than the emu and kangaroo paddocks'. Located within the well-kept grounds, a visit to the emus necessitated passing by the glorious view of the 'Capability Brown' lake, arriving at a rustic temple (one of many temples within the grounds) before turning left towards the woodlands and paddock. The emus themselves were fully acclimatised and lived year-round outside in the grounds, with the shelter of sheds for rest and procreation. Arriving at the paddocks accompanied by the old gamekeeper, 'Long', Frank Buckland encountered what he at first mistook for an old feather bed laying in a corner. This was 'Tom', the oldest male emu, who was determinedly sitting on eggs, whilst also raising three live chicks. The female emu, whose name Buckland did not record, had left the young ones in the care of the father, who took them out into the grazing areas, provided for them and protected them. Originally from Australia, the emus had been brought by the 7th Duke of Marlborough, John Winston Spencer Churchill, and handed to his gamekeeper in early May, along with a book on how to rear emus! Presumably originating from warmer climes than windswept England, this reference work had insisted that peaches and apricots were the ideal food for rearing emus. Even the best run of Victorian kitchen gardens lacked a profusion of these delicacies in early May, and faced with hungry emus the gamekeeper proffered spinach instead. 'Tom' apparently relished this, as did the younger emus once it was cut up finely enough. Bread and cakes were secondary tastes but spinach was 'what they is most partial to', as the innovative Long stated. The emus appear to have been tame enough to allow visitors into the paddocks, and the Duke hoped to increase the numbers and even perhaps populate the parkland. Re-capture however would have proved a problem, as the emus were said to be able to run extremely fast, certainly faster than the aged gamekeeper who had gout in one leg and rheumatics in the other.

FLAMINGO

The desire to have unusual and beautiful birds and beasts in the garden did not stop with the arrival of the late twentieth century, although ironically despite the easier and more rapid modes of travel, obtaining such living decoration became rather harder. The flamingos that still charm the gardens at Coton Manor were first introduced there in about 1975 by the father of the current owner. Known as 'the Commander' he had a home in the Bahamas and, admiring the beauty of the flamingos there, felt they would add some tropical colour to his Northamptonshire home. By the mid-1970s however, private individuals were no longer allowed to import these exotics, and Coton might have remained reliant on the more muted tones of our native bird population had it not been for the interest of the famous naturalist Peter Scott. Scott had a licence to import birds as part of his wetland bird sanctuary at Slimbridge, Gloucestershire and was interested in introducing Caribbean flamingos onto the site. Mr Pasley-Tyler therefore arranged for a large number to be sent to Slimbridge, in return for which he was given twenty individuals to keep at Coton. These deep salmon-pink Caribbean flamingos were soon joined in their Northamptonshire home by some paler pink ones from Chile and they lived in harmony of temper, if with a slight colour clash, for many years. The ageing population was bolstered from yet another continent in the mid 1980s, when the present owners (Susie and Ian Pasley-Tyler) bought two Greater Flamingos, a species that originates in Africa. Despite being born and bred in Buckinghamshire, the new arrivals did not feel sufficiently at home to kick-start the breeding programme that was hoped for, and at present the flamingo flock stands at seven, two of whom are from the original 1975 import. Perhaps the freezing winters have affected their breeding, as they skate around on the iced pond. Early escapes resulted in a regime of wing clipping, although neighbouring reservoirs and wildlife centres were quick to report an influx of unusual immigrants and all escapees were returned. The flamingo acquires its wondrous colour from a special shrimp in its diet in its native habitat, a shrimp naturally lacking in the ponds at Coton Manor. Rather than adding this to the ponds, and risking an outbreak of pink amongst the swans, ducks and geese that share the flamingo pond, the flamingo's characteristic colour is maintained by a feed supplement given in specially raised buckets stationed on the lawns. After the flamingos themselves it is the oddly placed feed buckets that arouse the most avid curiosity of the many garden visitors to Coton Manor, perhaps half convinced of a modern sculpture installation!

FLAMINGO II

Hidcote, the famous Gloucestershire gardens created by Lawrence Johnston, are famous for their rich colours and herbaceous borders. Lying to one side of the gardens is a woodland area, named after the Westonbirt Arboretum from which many of the trees came. From an unknown source came the startling pink flamingos that roamed the woodland of this archetypal English garden in the 1930s. Stalking the shrubberies, and striding through the maples, they shared their pool with cranes and a solitary ostrich. Perhaps unhappy with their dowdy woodland retreat they would periodically make a break for freedom, and several birds were lost before Johnston and his gardener Adams thought to clip their wings, obviously more used to pruning plants than forestalling flamingos.

GIANT TORTOISE

Rather different in scale to the traditional garden tortoise, the Galapagos Giant Tortoise can weigh up to 300kg (660lbs), with some individuals able to support the weight of a fully grown man on their backs. Rotumah, the pet tortoise at Tring, the home of the Hon. Walter Rothschild, weighed a comparatively meagre 300 pounds, although still able to carry his owner on short strolls around the grounds. Purported to be a 'centenarian twice over', he lived solely on the petals of flowers and vegetable foods, which carried him through the winter months without the need for hibernation. One of many animals which inhabited the grounds at Tring, (which Walter Rothschild developed as a small museum and zoo), the giant tortoise was said to be 'the one real pet'. Walter in fact funded and arranged several expeditions to the Galapagos for giant tortoise – hoping to obtain each of the different sub-species there, as well as a variety of other unique fauna and flora from the islands. Collecting the tortoises and lowering them onto the boats was extremely hard work, and it seems incredible (if unfortunate given the dwindling population) that twenty-nine live tortoises were eventually collected from the southern Galapagos islands of Charles, Albemarle and Duncan, and made the initial sea journey to San Francisco, as well as those which were collected as dead specimens. In San Francisco a greenhouse was rented for the recuperation of the giant animals ahead of their final sea journey back to England, and experiments made on keeping them alive on something other than their native cactus. Not content with this collection Walter was anxious to obtain the famed tortoise known as 'Rotumah'. In 1897 Rotumah

was residing in the gardens of a lunatic asylum in Sydney. Reported to be a most exotic and savage individual (perhaps accounting for its residing in the asylum). Rotumah was thought by Walter Rothschild to be a possible representative of a hitherto unknown species. This well-travelled beast had been liberated from its original island home in 1813 and taken to the Marquesas, before then passing through the ownership of King George of Tonga, who gave it to Mr Alexander MacDonald, who then housed it in the asylum gardens with the permission of Dr Manning the Government Inspector for Lunatic Asylums in New South Wales. Dr Manning offered to assist in accompanying Rotumah to his new home at Tring, and boarded *The Oceana* with the giant tortoise. A diet sheet and bill of sale was included, but despite these instructions (and the massive sum of £125 paid for the animal: equivalent to at least £3,000 today) poor Rotumah was left in the cold on the deck. Arriving at Albert Docks on 22 March, having sailed through the bitter February weather, the tortoise was stiff and seemingly lifeless. Arrival at Tring was just in time to save the giant and within a few days he was moving (slowly) around again. Photographs taken in the following months show Walter riding astride Rotumah, a cauliflower leaf dangling above the giant's head on the end of Walter's cane, in the manner of a donkey and carrot. Others show Rotumah exploring the grounds of the Museum, with flower borders forming decorative and edible backdrop. Alas Rotumah's mate had been left behind in the Sydney gardens, and despite the arrival of a photograph with which it was hoped to console him, Rotumah died of 'sexual over-excitation' two years later.

GOAT

Captain Cook's goat spent very little of her life in a garden until her deserved retirement as a pet at the Cook's family home. In the eighteenth century it was frequently the case that ships departing on long journeys would carry with them supplies including live hens and pigs. These animals would not only provide eggs or further pigs in the short term, but eventually be used as fodder themselves. Captain Cook's goat was unusual in already having served on a long distance ship, *The Dolphin*, before being loaded onto *The Endeavour* to set sail again. On *The Dolphin* she had accompanied Capt. Samuel Wallis and the explorer Tobias Furneaux, taking a westerly route to become the first Europeans (and the first goat) to reach Tahiti in 1767. Briefly back home, she was pressed into service by Captain Cook who departed in 1768 on his famous voyage of discovery across the Pacific in search of the southern continent. Stabled on the quarter-deck, the goat's needs and wants were probably catered for by one of the lowliest of the crew members, although the goat's modern biographer links her with thirteen-year-old Isaac Manley, a gentleman apprentice who would go on to outlive all the other crew members of *The Endeavour*. Captain Cook left a trail of goats behind him on each of his expeditions, seeing their proliferation as an insurance against food shortages on future visits, but his own personal goat he kept with him. After circumnavigating the world twice, providing fresh milk for the officers and gentleman for three whole years, and feasting upon previously unknown and untasted grasses of Tierra del Fuego, New Zealand and New Holland, the peripatetic goat arrived home to well deserved accolades and honours. She was awarded a silver collar by the Royal College, and the famous Dr Johnson was asked by Sir Joseph Banks, the eminent botanist who had accompanied Cook, to provide a suitable inscription for this. Writing to Banks on the 27 February 1772 Dr Johnson suggested the following: *'Perpetua ambitâ bis terrâ praemia lactis; Hoec habet altrici Capra secunda Jovis'*. Which was roughly translated by Johnson's friend Boswell as:

In fame scarce second to the nurse of Jove,
This goat, who twice the world has traversed around,
Deserving both her master's care and love,
Ease and perpetual pasture now has found.

Johnson explained that he had meant to recollect a motto from ancient times for the acclaimed goat, but odes to goats being scarce had had to make a new one up. Ease and perpetual pasture could have lasted quite some time, the normal life span for a goat being some 8–12 years. One hopes that she was only made to wear the heavy silver collar for best, and spent most of her retirement days in deliciously naked freedom. Her eventual demise was recorded retrospectively in the *Live Stock Journal* for New Zealand, and further reported in the *Transactions and Proceedings of the Royal Society of New Zealand* in 1902. Co-incidentally, Captain Cook's birthplace, a small cottage in Gt Ayton, North Yorkshire, fronted onto a track called Goat Lane: at least it did until 1933 when it was bought for £300 and moved to Australia!

GOLDFISH

Sir Robert Heron of Stubton Hall in Lincolnshire was one of the earliest breeders of goldfish in this country. Writing in 1814, he confides to his journal his love of his fish, which he had then been breeding for some six years. His collection was housed in a series of large paved ponds in his flower garden, which appear to have been heated. The (rather inappropriately named) Sir Heron, had originally obtained six fish from two separate sources, perhaps indicative of their rarity at this time, or an advanced realisation of the problems of in-breeding? A further two coal-black fish, supposed to have originated from a volcanic lake in China, were added to enhance the colour range in the pool, but much to his distress these immediately turned red. Despite the initial setbacks in obtaining different colours, the mysterious colour-changing fish gave birth to a range of descendants, and he was delighted to note that 'They certainly constitute a considerable variety from the ordinary sort'. A mix of black and red it may well be that these were not the standard Koi and the black 'Moors' but that he had managed to obtain something rare and unusual. Even his normal goldfish appear to have changed colour with unusual frequency, and he remarked that this 'uncertain and capricious' behaviour may have been linked to the changing of the water temperature in his heated ponds. By 1814 Sir Robert had a shoal of over eleven hundred fish, suggesting a larger 'garden pond' than is usually envisioned by the phrase! Sir Robert was obviously something of an obsessive with goldfish, as in addition to having eleven hundred in his own ponds, he also visited other people's ponds to examine their goldfish. Whilst visiting Sir

Charles Kent at Little Ponton, Sir Robert took the liberty of measuring his host's goldfish, which he discovered to be 12 inches long and 10 inches in circumference. The goldfish was thought to be of at least twenty-five years of age at the time of the visit, Sir Robert noting that the same fish had been alive in 1792. Still on the track of the elusive colour change, he noted that it was 'becoming paler than in its 'youth'. Back home, pausing only to record the Battle of Waterloo and his own election failures in his journals, Sir Robert recorded one morning having discovered a favourite (large white) goldfish under attack by a toad, which had fastened itself upon the head and shoulders of the fish, presumably mistaking it for a female toad. Leaping to the rescue Sir Robert detached and killed the toad, watching whilst the large white fish made good its escape. He killed over a hundred toads in the ponds that April, perhaps fearing further inappropriate advances. Heedless of the possible dangers of further inter-species sexual frustration, he also introduced Brazilian Tortoises into the aquarium, which must have added to already chronic over-crowding. Certainly this was not a garden pond likely to have sported lilies! In 1841 disaster struck in the form of a severe frost. About one hundred fish died from cold, something which he comments had never occurred before. In addition to his aquatics, Sir Robert's colourful collection of animals and birds also included armadillo, emus, kangaroos, rheas, guinea pigs, golden pheasants, red-cheeked parakeets, an albino cock, spotted dasyurus, a colour-changing chameleon, chequered starlings, and black swans, but one feels his heart lay with the goldfish.

GUINEA PIG

In their native South America these entertaining 'little pigs' are kept running loose in homes and gardens and a special occasion or honoured visitor is traditionally celebrated by the demise and consumption of one of these small house guests. In Europe they are more usually kept in hutches and runs in the garden, although some protection is needed from the winter weather and 'house pigs' are increasingly popular. The traditional European hutch was a rather boring wooden 'box' with wire front and bedding area, a fall from grace for an animal whom the Peruvian Indians once venerated with statues. For the guinea pigs of the Lamb family of Beauport Park a rather more elaborate domicile awaited. Inspired by a fascination with knights and chivalry, Charles (Charlie) Lamb (born 1815) created an entire kingdom for his 'pigs. The Kingdom of Winnipeg inhabited Cabbage Castle, a complex and ever expanding miniature citadel in the gardens of Beauport Park. Providing constant work for the estate carpenter, the walled city included castles, pyramidal tombs, columns, crenellated towers, gatehouse and ancillary 'offices'. Flags flew over the main city areas of Farai and Lelia, declaring the royal family and its 'dependants'. The history of this city state was recorded by young Charles in eight green and red leather volumes. As would be expected, the descendency and familial relations of the royal families were complex and fluid, with over a hundred guinea pigs eventually housed in Cabbage Castle. Most descended from the original King Geeny and Queen Cavia and their companions Sir Coccus Wallaia and Turkininede Newton, and the 'marriage' of the king with his own daughter might have caused some scandal amongst human aristocracy. The volumes in which the royal family's histories were diligently recorded were illustrated with guinea pigs in armour, watercolour portraits of the 'pigs, and illustrations of the crenellated and castleated residence, surrounded by the ancient landscape and towering trees of Beauport Park. Coats of arms were created for individual members of the aristocratic guinea pig family. For example one warrior knight was distinguished by the heraldic shield of 'Argent three rate keeled proper'. Despite their royal residence, life was not all roses for Charles Lamb's guinea pigs. In addition to the dysentery and consumption which their young keeper recorded as it afflicted them, the neighbouring rabbits (written by Charles as 'rarribuns') were apparently difficult neighbours, over-running the castle, breaking into and eating the food stores of cabbage and grain, and bullying its royal inhabitants. Despite sketches of 'pigs in armour and with shields, Charles never managed to actually get his royal inhabitants to joust, although his interest in them continued over almost a decade. Charles' half brother, Archibald, had better fortune when he arranged and (held) the Victorian revival of the medieval joust at the Eglinton Tournament of 1839. His brother Charles was part of the tournament, appearing as the Knight of the White Rose. The historian Ian Anstruther described Charles Lamb as a dreamy and artistic child, obsessed with knights and tournaments who lived entirely in a private world of shining knights and chivalry, to which one would have to add, guinea pigs.

GUINEA PIG II

Even garden designers have their weaknesses. Gertrude Jekyll had her cats and William Robinson his dogs whilst Berthold Körting favoured guinea pigs. A German landscape designer and architect of the 1920s, Herr Körting was based in Berlin. Here he developed a unique guinea piggery. Featured in *Modern Gardens British and Foreign 1926-27* and issued by the ultra-fashionable *The Studio* magazine the guinea pigs (and accompanying dovecote) could have set a fashion had European history been different. In contrast to the medieval glory of Beauport Park guinea pigs, Herr Körting's enjoyed a rococo style. An accompanying photograph shows a circular enclosure of low brickwork, entered by a scaled-down ornate gateway complete with what appears to be ornate ironwork 'piers' of suitable scale. The editor of *The Studio* commented that Körting's garden was 'interesting in its formality and suggestion of Japanese influence' but completely failed to mention the guinea pigs.

HARE

Leaving their leverets hidden in the fields during the course of the day, hares would often return to an empty 'nest' in the days before mechanisation, when the fields were the frequent haunts of village children. Once the children had become bored with their new 'toys' the leverets lives were usually short. Three such leverets however had the great fortune to be handed on to the eighteenth century English poet and hymn writer, William Cowper, who with his tender care and intuitive nursing, was able to rear all three to adulthood. Bess sadly died quite young but Puss and Tiney lived for over nine years, inhabiting both the house and garden. Puss in particular grew increasingly tame and affectionate towards his poet keeper, and, following a short illness which Cowper cured with a variety of herbs, Cowper made it his custom to carry the young hare into the garden every morning after breakfast. Once here, Puss would generally hide under the leaves of the cucumber plants, sleeping, 'chewing cud' (as Cowper described the complex system of caecotrophy) and nibbling at the cucumber leaves until evening. This habit established during his convalescence, Puss wished to continue it once he was well. Soon he took to drumming on Cowper's knees when he wanted to be taken into the garden, and if that hint was not taken he would 'take the shirt of my coat between his teeth, and pull at it with all his force'. Despite these signs of horticultural fervour, the hare was said to prefer human company to all others, showing distress when shut up with his natural companions. Tiney was not of such an affectionate disposition, and perhaps not trusted to return, had to make do with a Turkish Carpet indoors for his lawn, where he would skip and gambol. Cowper became greatly attached to Tiney and Puss, commenting on their intelligence and recording their individual characters. He came, he said, to hold the sportsman's amusement of hare coursing in abhorrence, knowing what enjoyment his charges had in life, their gratitude and their cheerfulness of spirit. This love he portrayed in his poem *The Garden* from which the following is an excerpt:

Well, one at least is safe.
One shelter'd hare
has never heard the sanguinary yell
of cruel man, exulting in her woes.
Innocent partner of my peaceful home,
Whom ten long years' experience of my care
Has made at last familiar;

On the death of Tiney the poet buried him beneath the walnut tree of the garden, and wrote a further poem in remembrance of the hare's beguiling nature, a nature that had so often forced him to a smile when he was otherwise in melancholy spirits.

I kept him for his humour's sake,
For he would oft beguile
My heart of thoughts that made it ache,
And force me to a smile.
But now beneath his walnut shade
He finds his long last home,
And waits, in snug concealment laid,
Till gentler Puss shall come

(*Epitaph for a Hare* by William Cowper: excerpt)

HEDGEHOG

When choosing an animal as a pet considerations usually include the satisfaction to be gained from physical contact with the animal. Soft fur, long silky hair, or downy feathers are favourite body coverings, producing a soothing and pleasant experience when stroking the pet. It is not surprising therefore that hedgehogs, with their covering of protective spines, provide rather fewer examples of garden pets than even the bear or the monkey. That indefatigable champion of pet ownership, Rev. Wood, had however amongst his correspondents a lady who had decided to make it her mission to domesticate the hedgehog. Purchasing her first hedgehog for the purpose of keeping the house free of cockroaches (surely a method which deserves to be re-introduced in these days of organic pest control), she discovered, by virtue of its giving birth the next day, that it was a female. Alas the upheaval immediately before its delivery of the babies was too much for it, and the babies all died. However fired with enthusiasm for the small animal, and forgetting the original purpose of the purchase, the lady decided to purchase a further (male) hedgehog and keep them as garden pets. The garden in question was some forty feet square, and presumably well walled. Giving her new cares an old kennel as a home and some cloth bedding they appear to have settled in contentedly. That autumn they were seen constructing a hibernating chamber of leaves behind one of the dustbins, where they were left undisturbed. A keen naturalist the lady owner weighed them before hibernation, and discovered the female to have gained considerable weight since the spring, now being two and a quarter pounds. The following June, of 1882, five or six little hedgehogs were discovered running about the grass on the lawn, which she guessed to be a month old. Experiments with food followed, perhaps in the realisation that even the most pest infested garden of forty foot square cannot hope to maintain an active (and growing) hedgehog family of eight. Eggs were a favourite meal, as were the titbits of liver, fat, biscuits, bread, butter and milk. Unsurprisingly this array of delicacies scattered through the garden also attracted many mice, and the owner was forced to start laying mice traps, feeding the victims to the hedgehogs. Ironically the very cockroaches that the hedgehog had originally been purchased to rid the house of were now elaborately caught by hand and, after being killed by boiling water, were taken out into the garden as feed. The observation that 'a hedgehog can eat as many as 200 cockroaches at one meal', would seem to confirm the writer's assertion that by now the kitchen was swarming with cockroaches, and one wonders why the hedgehogs were not just locked in the kitchens at night to carry out the unpleasant slaughter for themselves. A second litter was born in the garden the following year, but one after the other, the pet hedgehogs eventually succumbed to a variety of accidents and illnesses. Finally two of the younger ones were set free in nearby woods and another given to a friend as a garden pet, whilst the original female was given her liberty on 1 August 1883 in the village of Plumtree, being placed in a thick hedge close to a nice damp brook. Incidentally, for two years this same garden was also the home of a large pet toad belonging to the correspondent's mother, who was most distressed when her beloved animal was one night eaten by one of the hedgehogs who, we are told, made a noise 'as of someone eating in a vulgar manner' and was caught with the hind-legs still hanging from its mouth.

HEN

Many a gardener over the centuries has welcomed a few hens into the garden, putting up with their occasional unwanted depredations in the flowerbeds in return for a supply of fresh eggs. However, few hens have graced such palatial gardens as those kept by the Duchess of Devonshire at Chatsworth in Derbyshire. Spilling out from their adapted stone house in the five hundred year old parkland, the hens patrol the car park for signs of picnics and play daredevil with the car drivers. A great advocate of hen-keeping, the Duchess herself intro-duced hens into the gardens in the 1970s. She carefully chose the variety 'Buff Cochin' for their large feathered feet which make them less likely to scratch up seedlings and fragile plants; whilst their stately walk and attractive colours ornament the gardens around the potting shed. Other varieties wander-ing free-range at Chatsworth include Welsummers, White Leghorns, Silkies, and Marans, all pure breeds, and including some prize-winners at the Royal Show. The exotically named Appenzeller Spitzhaubens also make an appearance, having been introduced into England by the Duchess' sister. Poultry keeping runs in the Duchess's family, her mother having kept Rhode Island Reds and White Leghorns so successfully that she was able to pay the governess' wages for all her daughters with the profits. The Duchess keeps the hens for their interest and amusement, rather than for their indirect assistance in education, although as a supporter of the Poultry Club she also promotes their welfare through her writing. In the glorious setting of the gardens at Chatsworth the Duchess' hens are some of the most aristocratic poultry in the country, as well as the most frequently photographed.

HEN II

Vauxhall Farm in Tong, Shropshire is famous for its array of bizarre garden and farm buildings. Amongst these is the pyramidal henhouse. Built by Mr George Durant, the henhouse can be seen from the gates, and was carved with suitably informative inscriptions for the hens. These included 'Scratch Before You Peck', and 'Teach Your Granny' (how to suck eggs). A bas-relief of a cockerel was inscribed along with the words 'Egyptian Aviary 1842'. The carving of a cat carrying a kitten is slightly more mysterious – or perhaps ominous. Mr Durrant also had 10ft pyramids constructed over the gate piers of the house entrance, from where he used to preach *extempore* to passers by. Perhaps taking as his text Mathew 23 verse 27; 'how often would I have gathered thy children together even as a hen gathereth her brood under her wings'.

HYENA

If the records of the Amateur Menagerie Club are anything to go by, hyenas are a particular attraction to women, and an equally particular distraction to gardeners. Two articles in the 'Yearbooks' of this intriguing (and short-lived) club describe life with a domesticated hyena, and both are by women. Ebby, the striped hyena was the beloved pet of Rose Butler, whilst Squeaks, the spotted hyena, shared the home of Mrs Cogan. Whilst both were, by the accounts of their mistresses, un-equalled for affectionate natures, intelligence, good looks and entertaining accomplishments, Squeaks is the hyena who has the best claim on this book as he spent much of his time in the garden. Brought from West Africa as a baby, Squeaks was originally given the more distinguished and exotic name of Kui-Kui, but his attempts to produce the laughing noise that distinguishes his race resulted instead in the pathetic sounds that gave him his nickname. Lively and inquisitive the small bundle arrived with a covering of tawny grey fur, already spotted with black. He was soon pronounced 'absolutely tame' by his doting mistress and allowed to run loose about the garden, creating havoc with a terrier puppy as they had mock-battles amongst the flower borders. Mrs

Cogan appears to have been an unusual lady for the period not just in her choice of pets, but also in the fact that she did her own gardening. Reminiscent of more 'normal' garden pets, Squeaks would also 'help' gardening operations by variously sitting on the skirts of his mistress so that she could not move, or sitting just where she wanted to plant or sow something. He seized her trowel and gloves and would wander off and hide them like an overgrown mischievous puppy, which in many ways is exactly what he was, at that time being only the size of a bull-terrier. By the time he was 3 years old his gardening exploits became more reckless, and somewhat larger in scale, so that quite large shrubs would be dug up and carried off, whilst flower-beds were flattened by his rolling on them. Instead of banishing him from the garden, Mrs Cogan placed him on a long chain on the lawn, with enough room to 'scamper around' and with a large barrel to sleep in. As with most of the unlikely animals in this book, Mrs Cogan insisted that there was nothing Squeaks liked better than to be fondled and petted, although as well as licking his owner in return he would often 'pretend to gnaw ones hand or arm'. Perhaps it was similar 'pretend' gnawing that had restricted the garden life of Ebby, the striped hyena belonging to Rose Butler. Initially allowed the run of the walled kitchen garden his garden days were cut short when the head gardener informed Rose Butler that the men did not feel happy working in the garden whilst the hyena was loose. After that he was restricted in his garden strolls to those hours when the men were not working. Ebby would take the opportunity of these quiet moments in the garden to strip all the dwarf plum trees and soft fruits; not perhaps the outcome which the head gardener had desired but one that his mistress naturally thought of as endearing.

INDIAN ANTELOPE

A pair of these delightful creatures was kept by the Prince of Orange at his palace of Het Loo in The Hague in the mid-eighteenth century. In 1766 the pair was described by the naturalist Pallas, as displaying traits more usually associated with the 'ideal' eighteenth century human couple. The moralising Pallas described the male as somewhat wild at heart, although perfectly reserved and well-behaved in company, whilst the female of the pair was 'perfectly gentle and good tempered' with none of the wildness of the male. The female also took pleasure in being noticed, and would raise herself on her hind legs in order to get closer to people and demonstrate her affection, although her 'over-familiarity with strangers' would have been discouraged in her human counterpart. This familiarity may have had as much to do with the frequent hand-feeding of bread by her visitors as any innate desire for flattery and attention! Kept in an enclosure in the grounds of the palace, the pair would display their agility by racing at full speed, taking leaps of surprising lengths. Their decorative nature encouraged a later writer from the London Zoological Society to suggest that the Indian Antelope might prove a superior ornament and advantage to the parks and gardens of England, being more attractive than our present deer. The Society itself owned a single male specimen who was also reserved, but playful, butting its female (human) visitors with its horns. Analogies were not drawn in this case.

KANGAROO

The Queen's Cottage at the Royal Botanic Gardens, Kew, is a delightfully rustic thatched and timbered retreat. Built in the late eighteenth century, supposedly to the designs of Queen Charlotte herself, the cottage would look at home with a flock of English sheep grazing its lawns. In the 1790s however this peaceful paddock, in what was then Richmond Gardens, was home to a collection of prized kangaroos. Allowed to hop freely around the lawns, they were admired by Charlotte and her family when they came to take tea once a week in the decorated rooms of the cottage. In 1793, in a letter to Sir Joseph Banks, the King's apothecary (David Dundas) wrote that one of the female kangaroos had been 'if I may be allowed to use the expression, for some time in the state of parturition'. He continues 'I have taken the liberty to inform you that I learnt yesterday that the man who has the care of it had perceived the head of a young one appearing out of its pouch so long ago as 30 October'. Coyness was obviously not one of the traits of the kangaroos themselves, as the population rose to nearly twenty within the next ten years. The naturalist Shaw believed that their producing young would make the kangaroos 'a permanent acquisition in the country' being most elegant ornaments for English parks; although he was bound to admit that the alteration of food accompanied by any confinement, must make them display less of their natural habits and in particular 'exhibit somewhat less of that bounding vivacity which so much distinguishes them in the native wilds of Australasia'. In 1806 the still-bouncing kangaroos at Kew were dispersed to make way for a series of flowerbeds, returning the royal cottage to a rather more English appearance and less vivacity.

KANGAROO II

Almost a hundred years later the same experiment in adding 'bounce' to the English landscape was tried at Blenheim, the ancient home of the Dukes of Marlborough. Wisely kept in a paddock with high walls, rather than being lost to sight within the extensive Brown landscape, this small group again included females and their young, or as Frank Buckland, visitor to the park charmingly phrased it 'the lady kangaroos' and the little babies. On a less complimentary note he described the young as having 'rat-like heads' peeping out of the pouches. Buckland thought the kangaroos were a delightful and exciting addition to the landscape, and was anxious that kangaroos should be cultivated in all English parks as being very ornamental. However he also had an alternative motive. Oxtail soup being then a favourite dish, Buckland reasoned that the length and width of the kangaroo tail would provide a more substantial version of this meal! Having been informed by the Duke of Marlborough's kangaroo keeper that the animals were not destructive to plants and shrubs he felt they would indeed be ideal parkland animals. Even their habit of barking trees he felt could be easily broken and they could be encouraged instead to concentrate on grass. Although this sounds suspiciously like the optimism of the non-gardener! An unexpected difficulty to the Duke's kangaroo introduction in the park liberties was the tendency of the hunting hounds, so prevalent on estates of this kind, to route the small herd, causing the over excited 'roos to bound away in all directions. Still Buckland had every hope that one day the poem he had memorised at Oxford would be applicable to all English parks as much as to Australia, and that he would be able to declaim in his native landscape that: 'I love to climb the lofty hills and view; The untamed pastures of the kangaroo; Or, mid the gum trees' aromatic blossom, To watch the gambols of the young Opossum'. Alas, Blenheim at any rate does not seem to have harboured opossum.

LEMUR

William S Gilbert, one half of that famous comic operatic duo, Gilbert and Sullivan, had a weakness for pets matched only by his ability to include them within his witty rapport. An American reporter who asked Gilbert about a rumour that he was interested in cattle raising, was told, 'I have two thousand head of stock…principally bee'. The reporter is said to have innocently reported the two thousand head! Although in truth lacking in cattle, Gilbert's house and grounds at Grim's Dyke, near Harrow (Middlesex) contained such delights as Siberian Cranes and an (initially) lonesome gazelle. Gilbert would take the gazelle for walks around the croquet ground, later purchasing a stag called Florian to keep it company in his absences. In early June 1906 Gilbert went down to London with his wife, Nancy, to purchase two lemurs to add to their domestic hearth; all four of them catching the 5.20pm back from Euston much to the consternation of the commuters. After a short spell in relative captivity as house pets, the lemurs broke their bonds and escaped to freedom in the extensive grounds, spending several days there before being re-captured. From then on Gilbert often allowed the lemurs their freedom, and they would roam the gardens and house, causing upheaval in the dining room by consuming the nectarines and bananas laid ready for guests. The happy pair of fruit lovers rewarded Gilbert for his forbearance by giving birth to a baby in the late summer of 1904. Gilbert was on holiday in Italy at the time of the birth, but rushing back to the house on 10 October, the first thing he did was visit the proud parents and their new offspring. The baby was given the rather unexotic name of Paul, and from then on his growth and development were recorded in Gilbert's diaries. Unfortunately Paul only lived in this happy ménage for three years, dying in August 1907 just as Gilbert completed writing one of his most famous operas, *The Mikado*. Paul was buried in the grounds of Grim's Dike. Gilbert himself died just a few years later attempting to save a guest who was drowning in the ornamental lake. The posthumous tribute written in *Century Illustrated* chose to include photographs not just of the great man himself, but also of Paul the lemur sitting on the garden steps, a tribute to the bond between man and lemur.

LEMUR II

Few lemurs have resided in such splendour as that belonging to the textile magnates Stephen and Virginia Courtauld. Purchasing the ruins of the medieval palace and grounds of Eltham Palace, Surrey, in the 1930s, the couple created an art-deco mansion to rival the original Great Hall. Pink leathered chairs, gold plated taps and mirrored bathrooms all lay within the red brick building that, externally at least, complemented the original buildings. In addition to art-deco the Courtaulds were passionate about animals, having the black and silver entrance doors of their mansion decorated with animals and birds drawn from life at London Zoo. They also kept a wide variety of pets who lived in the house and the nineteen acres of gardens. Mah-Jongg (or Jongy) was purchased by the Courtaulds at Harrods in 1923 and lived with the Courtaulds for fifteen years, travelling with them and living in their various homes or on board the yacht. At Eltham he was granted an indoor room, suitably decorated with bamboo forest scenes and with a bamboo ladder to ascend to the upstairs Flower Room. The only lemur bedroom to be featured in *Country Life*! He was also captured on film, along with the Courtaulds other animals, relaxing in the gardens and sunning himself by the pool. Stephen Courtauld was a director at the Ealing Film Studios and so his ten-minute reels have that extra professional quality missing from most family home-movies. Jongy was not that popular with everyone, being famous (or infamous) for biting people he did not like, including on one notable occasion the expedition wireless operator for the British-Arctic expedition, the night before they were due to sail. The expedition had to manage without him for the next three months as he proved allergic to the iodine used to treat the bite. An expedition which Mah-Jongg himself did not miss was that of the Courtaulds in search of orchids. The Courtaulds were great orchid collectors and in the late winter of 1936/7 sailed around the South China Seas in search of new discoveries. Mah-Jongg of course went with them, relaxing in a jaunty stripy deckchair of his own, which complemented his stripy tail. On Mah-Jongg's death, at Eltham, a memorial was commissioned by the Courtaulds from the Gilbert Ledward, Professor of Sculpture at the Royal College of Art. The monument, placed in the gardens where he had enjoyed frolicking, comprised a banded obelisk in imitation of the lemur's tail, and a lead relief of 'Jongy', apparently biting his own tail. The memorial was eventually transferred to the Courtauld's new gardens at La Rochelle in Zimbabwe when they left Eltham in the 1940s.

LEOPARD

Archibald, 10th Duke of Hamilton kept a leopard at Hamilton Palace in the 1830s. At first it was allowed to roam the palace, but as it became more playful was relegated to the country estate of Chatelherault where, for the price of £8 3s 11d a small house was built for it in the grounds by the architects Messrs J.W. and G Fairley. The leopard house still exists in remarkably close vicinity to the main mansion, but its occupant is no more.

LION

Lions have always been associated with royalty, and Scottish royalty is no exception. The lion rampant on the Scottish flag gives support to the inclusion of lions in the collections of 'beastes and pettis' (beasts and pets) of many Scottish monarchs from Richard I to James VI. These beasts were usually kept in enclosed menageries in internal palace rooms, for instance at Stirling and Linlithglow, but the lions at Holyrood appear to have had a slightly wider reign. Here a lion yard and lion house were components of the palace grounds from at least the sixteenth century. In 1506 a lion was brought to be kept at Holyrood Abbey from Leith and payment made to an Andrew Broun (sic.) who kept the lion. In the late sixteenth century up to £244 a year was being expended on the feeding and keeping of the lions (along with a tiger and possibly a lynx). By then payment was being made to a Thomas Fentoun, who is recorded as being the keeper of the Palace Gardens. Head gardener in sixteenth century Scotland obviously included much more in the job remit than one might expect today! The exact whereabouts of the lions is uncertain as the Scottish term 'yard' may be translated either as a garden or an enclosed area for herbs etc. However accounts refer to the 'little garden where the lions are kept' so we may presume a securely enclosed space but with plants and greenery. A study of the history of the gardens at Holyrood has suggested that this area may have lain to the north of the Palace.

LION II

A Boston (Massachusetts) backyard is an unexpected place to find a pair of lions, but that is exactly where Martha and Willie passed much of their days. Originally born in a travelling menagerie, the young lions were made homeless at the age of three months when the menagerie split up. Passed to a Mrs Lincoln to raise, Willie and Martha survived, although their three siblings alas did not. Spending much of their time asleep, as well-fed lions will do, they favoured a position indoors on their mistress's bed. However their rough and tumble games were too much for the indoors and they spent many hours in the yard of the house, apparently even encouraging the cat to join in their romps. Still happily domesticated at the age of four the two must have looked rather out of place in nineteenth century Boston, and the inclusion of a more usual domestic cat in their midst can have done little to re-assure the neighbours. Perhaps they merely counted their blessings that premature death had resulted in only two lions in the yard, rather than the original family of five.

LIZARD

The horror with which gardeners almost invariably greeted unusual garden pets was frequently justifiable as chaos, destruction and even severe wounding might be expected to follow rapidly in their wake. However the prejudice shown by the Wood's family gardener on the matter of a pet lizard seems unreasonable. The young Theodore Wood, later the rather eccentric Reverend Wood, presented the gardener with his new pet with all the triumph that its capture merited. Rather than exhibiting the curiosity that had been expected the gardener apparently showed every sign of extreme horror. As the author of *Out of the Way Pets* recalled, 'The man was terrified almost out of his wits, and sprang backwards with a yell which would have done credit to an ordinary locomotive engine. He was literally shaking like a leaf, and was almost as white as the paper on which I am writing.' Describing the lizard as a 'nasty creature' the gardener claimed that lizards were the most poisonous things alive. Folklore apparently ascribed to them the habit of living in hayfields, and waiting until the haymakers were having their post-prandial snooze, the lizards would creep up on them and bite them. 'And then', the gardener continued, 'the pore fellers as is bitten they goes on swellin' and swellin' until they busts!' The trusty, if gullible, employee, begged his young master to throw away his new pet before it could do him any mischief. Wood's response, to place his finger in the mouth of the lizard, did not soothe the worried gardener, despite the subsequent lack of swelling and death. That he had escaped with his life was regarded as both a mystery and a marvel. The gardener was not alone in his prejudices and apparently the 'average peasant' (as Wood rather condescendingly put it) believed lizards were of the most venomous description with depths of malignity, possibly acting as direct emissaries of the powers of darkness. It was only the rapidity of the lizard's movements and its habit of dwelling in secluded haunts that saved it from extinction by over-zealous gardeners. This particular lizard was saved by its young owner from an unjustified death, but not henceforth allowed to wander freely in the garden.

LLAMA

It would be surprising, indeed disappointing, if one of the earliest Presidents of the Royal Society for the Prevention of Cruelty to Animals (RSPCA) were not to have made an appearance in a book on pets. Baroness Angela Burdett-Coutts (1814–1906) is perhaps less well known today than she deserves. Daughter of Sir Frances Burdett, who was responsible for the passing of the Martin Act of 1822, the first ever legislation protecting animals, Miss Burdett-Coutts led an active social and campaigning life. One of the wealthiest heiresses in the country (inheriting the wealth of the Coutts banking family on changing her name) she was active in schemes addressing many of the 'ills' of Victorian England, including 'fallen women', education of the poor, temperance movements, prevention of cruelty to children, missionary work, lifeboats, and seed-donation to rural poor. A close friend of Charles Dickens, and an even closer 'friend' of the Duke of Wellington (whom it was rumoured she secretly married) it comes as a surprise that she had any time for domestic life. Her home at Holly Lodge was the centre of her social and domestic circle, and here she kept the animals that formed for many years her closest 'family'. A small *ferme ornée* sprung up spontaneously with a herd of prize-winning Anglo-Nubian goats, champion pigs, and a sleek white Egyptian donkey. Most unusually she also kept two pet llamas which grazed on the lawns overlooking the Surrey hills and the London suburbs. The llamas had been brought from Peru by Sir Spencer St John, British Ambassador there, at the instigation of Miss Burdett-Coutts. As with many of her designs this was again linked as much with alleviating poverty as pet owning, as she had heard of an experiment by Sir Titus Salt, a Bradford wool merchant, that a handsome alpaca cloth could be made of the wool. If the llamas could be introduced and bred in this country then, she reasoned, they might be ideal for small rural industries of weaving which could be set up with a pair of these unusual animals. The two forerunners arrived, joining the collection of dogs, parrots and donkeys at Holly Lodge and formed a decorative feature on the lawn; where they were depicted on an invitation card to a reception in 1867. As with so many schemes to introduce foreign animals, this too was doomed to failure as the llamas declined to breed and remained ornamental rather than functional, providing wonder rather than warmth and remaining resolutely un-industrious. Her presidencies of the National Goat Society and National Bee Keeping Associations led to more practical success amongst the needy, and the llamas finished their days stuffed in glass cases. Angela Burdett-Coutts was, incidentally, also responsible for raising the statue to the famous Greyfriars Bobby in 1872, a testimony to the dog's faithfulness.

MARMOSET

Norah L. Walker, correspondent to the Amateur Menagerie Club in 1926, was besotted with monkeys of all kinds. Inheriting her 'monkey-mania' from her mother, who had had a similar weakness, Norah was in an excellent position to advise others on the various merits of monkey keeping. Most of the monkeys were kept indoors, but marmosets she claimed could be easily kept in a 'wired in bush' in the garden over summer, and then allowed the run of the garden conservatory in winter. In fact her own were over-wintered in the kitchen where they usefully caught flies, and also gave birth. Perhaps a case of 'a marmoset in the kitchen being the sum of two in the bush'?

MONKEY

Writer of numerous books on botany and gardening for women and children, the nineteenth century author Jane Loudon also branched out into works on domestic pets and nature study. *The Young Naturalists Journey*, describing the travels of herself and her daughter in search of plants and animals, combined all of her specialities. In addition it introduced her readers to Mrs Loudon's very own unusual pet, a monkey called Ungka. Ungka originally lived with his owner Mr Trelawney in a small cottage by the River Dart along with a selection of other animals, including a lemur, a chameleon and a white rat. This Malayan monkey with its beautiful jet-black hair and an expressive face, attracted the attention of Jane and her daughter Agnes, who fell in love with the creature, Mrs Loudon going so far as to declare Ungka ' a beautiful exemplification of the Almighty wisdom'. Ungka returned the compliment and apparently became firmly attached to Agnes, perhaps sensing an opportunity for escape from the more raucous confines of Mr Trelawny's crowded house. As old men will do, Mr Trelawny gave into the pleas of the young Agenes and on their return to their suburban home at Porchester Terrace, London, Ungka accompanied the Loudons. A small kennel was constructed for Ungka in the garden, and here he lived through the summer months, taking shelter under the veranda and playing with their other pets, Sandy the cat, and Fairy the dog. Together they would run races with little Agnes. The gardens at Porchester Terrace were used by Jane

Loudon's husband, John Claudius Loudon, as 'model gardens', scrupulously neat examples of his best-selling work on *The Suburban Gardener and Villa Companion* and it is a testimony to his love for his only daughter that he allowed a monkey, a cat, a dog and a child to run rampant in the neat flowerbeds, in which 3,000 species were represented. In the harsh Victorian winters Ungka was brought indoors to live in the library and a small red flannel jacket made for him by him by his devoted owner. In fact Mrs Loudon may well have come to regret Ungka as, although she claims in her 1840 book never for a moment to have regretted the adoption of Ungka; by 1851 she writes that 'monkeys are not very agreeable domestic pets as they are extremely fond of mischief and frequently vicious and spiteful to children. In addition, she continues with an aggrieved air, they will steal goldfish either from a bowl or shallow garden pond if given the opportunity and thus need constant watching. As Jane had also written lovingly of her tame goldfish, who would come to feed from her own hands, one suspects Ungka had blotted his copybook.

MONGOOSE

Faced with that perennial unwelcome inhabitant of kitchen gardens, the rat, most gardeners bring in a cat or two to keep the rodent population at bay. In the case of Ellen Willmott (1858–1934) of Warley Place, Essex, the solution was not so pedestrian. Instead, one of her hundred-strong team of uniformed gardeners, a Mr Potter, was equipped with a pet mongoose with which to devastate the rat population. The mongoose, and Mr Potter, were captured by Miss Willmott on camera in the last decade of the nineteenth century, the mongoose scenting the air as it perches on Mr Potter's shoulders. Should the mongoose have been derelict in its duties, Miss Willmott might have contemplated the Tiger Bittern as an alternative, as the naturalist La Borde assured his readers that the bird had the dexterity of a cat in the catching of these rodents. Despite being kept as a garden pet for two years however the bittern in question was still in the habit of concealing itself around corners of the garden and assuming a threatening air whenever it was approached. Perhaps the mongoose was a better bet after all.

MOOSE

It is not an infrequent occurrence that the owner of a beloved pet will have its portrait painted for posterity and the walls of English galleries are hung with loving portrayals of horses and dogs. The National Portrait Gallery, London, has even published a book called *The Face in the Corner,* about the pets to be seen peeping out of people's portraits. The Duke of Richmond's moose did not so much peep coyly from a corner, as dominate the entire canvas. The moose was one of a considerable collection of animals that the 3rd Duke kept at his seat of Goodwood House, Chichester. The collection had been started by the 2nd Duke, who had kept bears, tigers, wolves and monkeys, as well as a favourite lioness, who was immortalised as a life-size stone statue, erected above her burial place in the park. By the time of the 3rd Duke, the collection was considerably diminished, and the moose (actually a series of mooses) was singled out as a particular 'pet'. The naturalist Gilbert White, writing in his journal in 1770, recalls a visit to Goodwood in March 1768 during which he was fortunate enough to see a female moose there, although as she had died literally the day before one could not credit him with having seen a live moose. Gilbert White was not very complimentary about the moose, recording that 'the ears were vast and lopping, and as long as the neck; the head was about twenty inches long, and ass-like; and had such a redundancy of upper lip as I never saw before, with huge nostrils'. It also had a dreadful stench, despite only having been dead a single day. In common with so many of his contemporaries, the Duke had great hopes of acclimatising and breeding these exotic animals in England. To breed, one needs more than a single moose, and the female that White described was at first accompanied by a partner which had died in the spring of 1767, although rather confusingly White states that this was also a female. The importation of two females appears at first puzzling but it might have been part of the Duke's plan for acclimatisation, as he had placed a young red deer stag in the garden with the moose in the hope that they would cross breed. This they failed to do, and the world was robbed of a Moer or a Doose! The Duke then obtained from the Governor-General of Canada a bull (male) moose, probably the first ever in the country. The moose appears to have been exceptionally affectionate and docile, with a sincere attachment to his carer, who fed him apples and stroked his nose and throat. His slow gait (the moose not the keeper) gave him an air of thoughtfulness and gravity which appealed to all who saw him. Samuel Johnson described the moose as more intelligent than horses of a similar age, although rather too apt to trustingly follow strangers if they proffered him an apple. It was this bull-moose that George Stubbs was commissioned to paint. A year old

in 1770, the moose is shown with realistically short antlers, but a mature set of antlers, possibly those shown to Gilbert White on his visit to Goodwood, are placed in the picture to give an indication of what is to come. In fact the artist was commissioned not by the Duke but by the surgeon William Hunter, (brother of John Hunter: see Z for Zebu), himself a collector of animals and birds, alive and dead. The portrait, he told Stubbs, should portray an 'exact resemblance' of the animal, to enable him to distinguish whether it was the same species as the extinct Irish elk. In 1773 the Governor-General presented yet another moose to the Duke, this time a two year old male, and the portrait of the original male was taken back to Goodwood by Hunter to see what difference maturity made to the species. Three things may be surmised from this short history: Firstly that the Duke had a soft spot for moose, secondly that they did not live long in his care, and thirdly, that as a prospective breeder he seems to have spectacularly failed in appreciating the importance of having a pair of the opposite sex!

MUNTJAC DEER

Most walkers or ramblers in the counties of East Anglia and the Midlands will be familiar with the muntjac deer, or to give it its full title, the Reeve's or Chinese Muntjac. So familiar have these small, rotund, animals become that some people even assume they are native to this country. However their introduction relies on yet another pleasure ground. This time it was the Duke's of Bedford who decided that the muntjac would beautify their Woburn Estate in Bedfordshire. Reeves Muntjac derive their name from John Reeves, who was appointed Assistant Inspector of Tea for the East India Company in 1812, and toured China and Asia, where the muntjac are indigenous. When the 11th Duke, Herbrand, first imported them, he included not only the Reeve's but also the true Indian Muntjac, however it is rumoured that an Indian Muntjac was responsible for the death of one of the Duke of Bedford's favourite dogs and so the small group at Woburn Abbey was destroyed. It must therefore be assumed that any muntjac seen in the wild around Bedford today will be a Reeves Muntjac. Herbrand's wife, Mary, dutifully catalogued the births and deaths and escapees amongst the small (but growing!) colony up until 1914, and there are specific records of the release, or escape, of nine immature females into the countryside around Woburn. Even with a very successful adaptation and breeding rate this could not possibly account for the current wild population of about 40,000 and others must also have escaped from parks and pleasure grounds that had followed in the Duke's footsteps. In 1942 the Duke himself wrote an article for the Royal Society of London on the incredibly successful year-round breeding of the muntjac on the estate, blissfully unaware of the problems these were to cause when they made their escape. Mary, the careful chronicler, met a more mysterious end, disappearing whilst on a solo flight in a de Havilland Gypsy Moth plane at the age of seventy-one.

NIGHTINGALE

The startlingly beauteous song of the nightingale will resound through any garden lucky enough to be visited by these melodic birds. In the past many people have sought to capture the song by imprisoning the birds themselves in cages and hanging them from the boughs of trees in pleasure gardens, giving rise to endless 'bird cage' walks. Beatrice Harrison had no need of such devices at her garden of Foyle Riding in Limpsfield, Surrey, as it was already home to these night-time performers. The songbirds at Foyle Riding were to be unexpectedly joined by a human accompaniment, for Beatrice was a professional cello player. Practicing the *Chant Hindou* by Rimsky-Korsakov in the garden one night, Beatrice was thrilled to have her playing echoed and extended by the nightingales, the bird's song following her in thirds as she trilled up and down the cello. Beatrice soon discovered that by playing certain pieces she could almost guarantee a response. She persuaded John Reith, the then

general manager of the BBC, to arrange an outside broadcast in her garden, and at midnight on 19 May 1924 the first ever duet for nightingale and cello was broadcast live. Over a million people listened to the broadcast, some having it played down the 'phone by friends with radio sets and loudspeakers! Its popularity was such that for the next twelve years the BBC recorded her live nightingale concerts every May. Thousands of (human) visitors also flocked to Foyle Riding to experience the garden concerts and, surprisingly, this did not appear to deter the nightingale accompanists who continued to donate their performances. Beatrice's sisters and parents were also musical, her sister May played violin, Margaret piano, and Monica was a singer. The family invited their musical friends to the nightingale concerts, as they were known, and even chartered buses to bring people from the East End, giving them tea and beer until midnight. Beatrice took the nightingale as her motif, depicting them on her concert posters and even embroidering the, rather dull looking, birds on her concert dresses. She also arranged a Nightingale Festival in aid of the Royal Society for the Protection of Wild Birds, which was then backing a bill in parliament to prevent blinded skylarks being sold in the East End markets, The garden was obviously inspirational, as it was here that the composer Delius had also commenced writing his cello concerto in 1923, alas without a part for nightingales. The Harrison family also kept parrots dogs, cats and fish, but fortunately did not broadcast any accompaniment they may have provided. Gerry the donkey who was with them from 1923 into the 1950s, may well survive on tape somewhere in the archives of the BBC, as he provided a prelude to the first ever nightingale recordings by constant braying as the sound engineers attempted to set up their delicate equipment. The only person who it seems was discomfited by the performances was the good old gardener who one day declared to Beatrice 'I loves your music Miss, but I do wish it didn't attract them birds the way it do. They eats up all the fruit something cruel'.

ORANG-UTAN

To keep pelicans in a pond, and even tree frogs amongst tree ferns, seems in some ways understandable. But an orang-utan in an Orangery? However tempting the headline, and several newspaper articles have found it so, the truth is alas not quite as poetical. Whilst Lord Shelbourne, of Bowood, Wiltshire, did have an orang-utan and an orangery, the animal was actually kept in a part of the 'Orangery Wing' of the house, rather than in the hothouse itself. Specifically built by the architect Robert Adam, the eighteenth century 'Orangery Wing' included both an orangery and an area specifically designed to hold wild animals, including the orang-utan and a leopard (which had the privilege of being stroked by Jeremy Bentham, the famous philosopher and social reformer). A bear was also documented as being resident either here or in another part of the grounds. The animal enclosures opened onto the stable court, an arrangement terrifying for the more usual inhabitants of the stables, with false windows onto the south front garden. Perhaps it might have been better to establish the orang-utan in the Orangery, as it died from lack of heat one cold winter, a fate not shared by the oranges. The former menagerie and stables now house a gallery of sculptures, which are not so demanding in their requirements.

OTTER

In 1865, when the 5th Lord Braybrook decided to create a Pond Garden at Audley End, he was responding to the fashion for the romantic. Accordingly rugged rock-faces and gushing torrents were created by the careful manipulation of sluice gates and the purchase of some of James Pulham & Sons best artificial rock. Soon a small, but picturesque, imitation of the Lake District was fashioned in the rather tamer landscapes of Essex, sandwiched between the Earl's kitchen garden and the old 'Capability' Brown parkland. Somehow rocks, water and ferns were just not enough, and in 1867, whilst Lord Braybrook was on a fishing trip in Ireland, he decided to purchase an otter to add that extra picturesque touch. Rather predictably, given its Connemara origins, the otter was called Paddy (despite being female). A central 'ottery' was constructed to one side of the Pond Garden, and the otter entered her lodge through an entrance arch in the north wall of the pond. A further hatch in the footpath of the garden gave the otter keeper access to the lodge. To help Paddy to feel at home, a fountain was constructed in the centre of the otter pond (again of artificial rock) to imitate a natural mineral spring. This 'spring' was planted with ferns and mosses and doubtless fooled more visitors than it did otters. The captured and domesticated Paddy was said to have lived for over thirty years, although one might suspect a series of Paddys. The original (or only!) Paddy was eventually stuffed and placed amongst the large collection of taxidermy animals and birds in Audley End house where she may still be seen. Otters were relatively popular garden pets in the Victorian

era, when otter-hunting often resulted in the discovery (indeed creation) of young orphan otters. The eccentric Frank Buckland, one time Inspector of Fisheries, was able to fill an entire chapter of his book *Notes and Jottings on Animal Life* with tales of pet otters, with several originating from Ireland and often called Paddy. Victorian pet owners were, it seems, largely unimaginative.

OTTER II

Frances Pitt (1888–1964) kept two otters named Moses and Aaron in her Wiltshire garden. Named from having been found as babes in the bulrushes, on gaining adolescence they were found to be both female and became Madam Moses and Miss Aaron.

PARROT

James Shirley Hibberd, Victorian garden writer on all things of 'taste', kept at his suburban London home, parrots, cockatoos, parakeets, macaws and toucans, as well as a tame jackdaw and a flock of Angora goats. A parrot lover, his own featured on the frontispiece of his most influential work, *Rustic Adornments for Homes of Taste*, a title which competed only with his previous *Brambles and Bay Leaves: Essays on Things Homely and Beautiful* for the title which best epitomises the Victorian era of home and garden design. Hibberd had a favourite green parrot which lived with him for many years 'in the full enjoyment of his liberty', as Hibberd said, in the house and gardens in Stoke Newington. The parrot would spend his days perching in the lilac tree, driving away cats and sparrows by his croaking and diving. When hungry it would fly to its feeding bowl rather than eating any of the greens in the garden. This was a distinct advantage over the tame magpies and jackdaws that also haunted the Stoke Newington gardens, who were said to punish the amateur gardener by their destructiveness. Their great delight being to pull up every small plant by the roots and lay it out in the sun to perish, a process which Hibberd noted 'makes a wonderful change in the aspect of a gay border in the course of just an hour of two'. Wonderful being used here in its original meaning of something to wonder at, rather than something to rejoice in! The parrot on the other hand confined himself to wandering in the garden, traversing the lawns, and admiring the plantings. With typical Victorian ingenuity, and love of making one thing do two tasks, Hibberd recommended that a parrot house in the garden might be made to combine with a vinery 'where under the shadow of purple grapes, a large number of choice birds would find sufficient room to be happy'. His illustration for the design shows an elaborate structure in the Moorish style, complete with trellises, dome, arabesques, finials etc. A collection of parrots and parakeets would, he claims, have a splendid effect in such a building, and give it a truly oriental appearance. Further trellises would close it off for the winter and give it an even more impressive appearance. Given the parrots love of fruit, one suspects there might be less impressive show of grapes. The technical term for a parrot fancier is, by the way, a 'Psittacinephile' and the collective noun for parrots is a 'pandemonium'!

PEACOCK

As discordant as they are decorative, peacocks are usually reserved for the larger or more remote gardens where their cries may be tempered by their distance. Lady Julia Lockwood, Victorian author of the typically moralistic children's work, *Instinct; Or Reason? Being Tales and Anecdotes of Animal Biography* took this to extremes in keeping her pet peacock in her garden in Malta, whilst she spent her summers in England. Her peacock obviously forgave such treatment as it would come to greet her at Sa Maison, stopping part way along the Long Walk to spread out its magnificent tail for her. His reward was a portion of the bread that she kept in her garden-apron to feed her fan-tailed pigeons. Unlike the fantails the peacock was permitted to take his own bread direct from the pocket. As with many faithful pets of the Victorian age, the peacock was said by the servants to have pined away and died whilst his mistress was away from Sa Maison. Even the exceptionally sentimental Lady Lockwood had doubts over this show of faithfulness, suspecting instead that he had fallen foul of local pigeon shooters or the 'greediness of the Maltese servants'. Lady Lockwood consoled herself in her Maltese paradise with her dolphin fountain, gold and silver fish, orange trees, hibiscus, daturas and jasmine, and a vine that apparently rivalled that at Hampton Court.

PEACOCK II

The call of the peacock was also to be its downfall at that most bohemian of gardens, 16 Cheyne Walk. Not content with his jackasses, armadillos and wombat, Dante Gabriel Rossetti also attempted to introduce peacocks into the assembled garden 'chorus'. However their shrill trumpetings were the final straw for many nearby residents, clashing as they did with the lower bark of the jackass. Representations were made to the landlord, Lord Cadogan, and complaints were so numerous that the birds had to be got rid of. A possibly unique property clause was then added to the leases of Lord Cadogan's properties that 'no peacocks should be kept in the gardens of tenants'. The neighbours were not the only ones who appear to have taken umbrage at the peacock. A graceful, and otherwise timid, fallow deer who had the misfortune to arrive at the same time as the peacocks were in residence, followed the male around the gardens, stamping on every feather of the wondrous bird's display. The extraordinary inclusion of the 'no peacock' regulation came just in time, as in August 1865 Rossetti had written to inform his mother that 'the pea hen has hatched out two of her four eggs, and now stalks about with two little whining quernesses at her heels, no bigger or brighter than ordinary chocks, but perhaps a little steadier on their pins'. And, one might add, somewhat more vocal.

PEAFOWL

In 1813, in the midst of the Napoleonic War, Sir Robert Heron wrote despairingly in his journal of the political machinations of the French Emperor and the Russian campaigns. Should the Allies yield? Will the French Governor give up Italy? Ought England aid the return of the Bourbons? Relief from these worldly concerns was to be found at home in Lincolnshire amongst his peafowl and his fish. Peafowl had been his hobby for at least eleven years, and one which he attended to closely. These were not an un-named and faceless collection, but one in which (as he recorded) 'each individual differs in temper . . . as much, almost, as human beings'. Some made good fathers, some good mothers, others good lovers. Indeed one particular pied cock was so popular, Heron noted, that when confined for a while behind 'trellis walls' the hens still queued up for his attentions, spurning those of a young upstart japanned cock who courted them fruitlessly. Whilst their old favourite was still in view they remained faithful. They were rewarded at last by his release into the garden in late autumn, when, with Robert Heron watching, 'the oldest of the hens instantly courted him, and obtained the proofs of his love in my presence'. Alas such constancy did not hold when next year the cock was confined in the stables, when the old adage 'out of sight out of mind' held sway, and the japanned cock gained the field.

Sexual advances, Heron noted, are always made by the female of the species and it was the females he blamed for the inconstancy. Cock (or rather hen) watching also allowed Heron to note the variety of care taken by the hens of their broods, and the occasional attachments shown to those broods by the males. Keeping of peafowl was an aristocratic pleasure in the early nineteenth century, and Robert Heron made note of several other flocks kept by friends and neighbours including Lord Brownlow, Lord St John (who had a hen of twenty-three years of age), Sir John Trevellyan (who kept wonderfully alliterative 'perfectly plain peafowl') and Lady Chatham, from whom Heron obtained his own. Allowed to wander freely the peafowl apparently did best when not tamed to too great an extent. If they were allowed to become dependent on feeding they would start to hang around the house and open garden areas, becoming easy prey for the dogs and foxes. Sir Robert solved this dilemma of desire to watch set against losses to predators by installing an aviary for his peafowl in the garden close to the house. His fascination became so much that he continually added to his collections, and by the time of his death in 1854 not only had peafowl and goldfish (his original loves) but also lemurs, kangaroos, llamas, alpacas, jerboas, armadillos, agoutis, porcupines, Angora rabbits, capybara and the wonderfully named *bettongia pencillata* – also known as the bettong or woylie for short.

PECCARY

Those in search of a really affectionate garden pet need look no further than the peccary, according to the animal lover J. Delacour; whose two pet peccaries were apparently the most demonstrative and loving of all his (numerous) animals. Following the shooting of their mother in December 1921, this pettable pair were caught in St Laurent du Maroni, (French Guyana) when no larger than hedgehogs. In the following April they were transported back to France by boat, spending their time following their new owner around the deck and already evincing numerous signs of tameness and intelligence. Fortunately they awaited their arrival at their new home, the Parc de Clères, Normandy (France), before also demonstrating their ability to swim. Allowed to roam free throughout the park the peccaries would run full pelt back towards Monsieur Delacour when he came to visit them, even swimming through the lake if this formed the quickest route. Once they achieved their gaol they would rub their necks against his legs, wanting to be petted and stroked. At night these seemingly ultra-intelligent animals would retire to their 'little house' in the grounds, were, we are told, they knew perfectly well how to shut the door behind them, and open it again the next morning. Unlike boars they did not forage and dig, but left undisturbed the immaculate park grounds and lived happily side by side with the other inhabitants (wallabies, muntjac and Patagonian Cavies) in this pre-lapsarian Eden. In addition to their love of humans they were also fond of grass and leaves, and were fed on dog biscuit, bran mash and corn every day. 'Easily matching the best of dogs' these perfect pets do not appear to have been rewarded with names, or perhaps their gushing owner retained some sense of the embarrassment that might be caused should he perhaps reveal a preference for Pinky and Perky? A note of warning should perhaps be added, as modern sources claim that peccaries cannot be domesticated, and may be harmful to humans.

PELICAN

'A fowle between stork and a swan' was how John Evelyn described his first sighting of the pelican at St James's Park in February 1665. The pelican in question had been given to King Charles II as a 'restoration' present by the Russian ambassador and had been housed on the king's new canal there. Pelicans live for about twenty years, and over the centuries the tradition of eastern ambassadors giving replacement pelicans caught on, and the park maintained its population of these ungainly waterfowl. Dependent perhaps on diplomatic relations with the east, the numbers in the park have fluctuated but over forty different individuals have passed through the park just in the twentieth century. During the 2nd World War the (then three) pelicans were referred to as the Chiefs of Staff, although whether for their sagacity or ponderous looks is unknown. In 1977 the ambassador of Astrakhan presented two pelicans, called Astra and Khan. In 1995 two pelicans were brought from Prague Zoo to boost low numbers. Vaclav and Rusalka joined a white pelican and an Eastern white pelican already there. Their arrival prompted questions in the House of Lords as to the sex of the pelicans, the possibility of the patter of little webbed feet, and the desirability of installing pelican crossings within the park. Although Lord Inglewood assured the House that the pelicans had been sexed before their departure from the zoo (a male and female), their Lordships were sorry to hear that the pelicans in the park have not laid a fertile egg in the 300 years that they have been there. Pelicans it seems need a colony of at least ten before they will

produce young. This was heartening news for the other waterfowl in St James's however, as once the population of pelicans rises above four, their Lordships were told that they begin to act belligerently and consume the other young birds. This fact was sadly born out when, numbers having risen to five in October 2006, a pelican picked up and ate a pigeon. The unfortunate bird struggled in the pelican's enormous mouth for twenty minutes before being swallowed whole. His misdemeanour was not the first, as Percy the Pelican from Louisiana had caught and eaten a moorhen in the park in 2004 in front of some distressed American tourists from his home state. A Royal Parks official commented that 'This could have happened for a variety of reasons: offended dignity, bad temper, playing to a gallery of Americans. Perhaps he did it for entertainment'.

PENGUIN

Birds Eye Foods Ltd (now Birds Eye Walls Ltd) are famous for their frozen foods. In particular, as thousands of children would attest, their fish-fingers. In the summer of 1962, with much of their instant food success still ahead of them, they moved into a new headquarters at Walton-on-Thames, Surrey. Here they not only created a prestigious new office for their staff of six hundred, but also a four acre landscaped garden. Imposing itself on a pleasant suburban street, the front façade met the ground in a long rectilinear pool, or moat, overlooked by the director's offices. Tall perspex tubes filled with colourless anti-freeze made columnar bubble fountains and a sculpture of rising birds terminated the north end of the pool, accented by boulders, reeds and water lilies. Pools also graced the two inner courtyards, the west in Japanese theme. Just a few years later in 1965, the then Chairman (the rather aptly named Mr J Parratt) decided that the landscaped grounds were lacking in life and movement, and instructed his architects to seek out exotic birds and reptiles to embellish the silent pools. Soon they were scouring London and Chessington Zoos for inspiration, considering Caiman alligators, seals, pelicans and gannets. But it was the zoo's famous penguin pools which were to catch their eyes. By July 1965 the first pair of penguins had arrived in Walton-on-Thames from the Falkland Islands, accompanied by a fresh consignment of herrings from the Birds Eye wet fish processing plant at Lowestoft. Unfortunately the herring proved too large for the penguins, and had to be replaced with sprats from a different source. Unused to this new diet, the penguins at first had to be force-fed by hand, an unusual career change for the Establishment Manager, L.C. Sandells. By October a second pair of penguins had arrived, and plans were being made for the creation of shelter sheds over the winter. Concrete huts were built as housing for the penguins, and the flamingos that had joined them in the August of that year. Penguin ramps were installed around the pools that obscured the modernist design of the courtyard. Finally obliterating any pretence of clinically precise landscaping, chicken-wire screens were also eventually installed to keep out dogs and vermin. By 1967 the menagerie had expanded and the penguins were joined by four flamingos (two Cuban and two Chilean) and two Mandarin Ducks in the Japanese Court, whilst four Caiman alligators, two snapper turtles and two terrapins basked under infra-red lamps in the under-stairs interior pool. In 1969 two pairs of

Gentoo penguins were forwarded from the Falkland Islands, via Montevideo and then Frankfurt, before arriving in suburban Surrey. Here they joined four Humboldt penguins, and three Gentoos already in residence. The collection was not without its problems, even ignoring the effect on the gardens. The penguins in the Monolith Garden suffered from cracked feet, whilst in 1973 one managed to eat a length of electrical cabling. The alligators were rather too frisky for some visitors, who turned up for meetings in a more agitated and nervous state than was helpful for business. It also proved impossible to keep live fish in the moat, which rapidly became 'polluted' and lifeless (other than with its numerous penguins and flamingos), and it seems a miracle that there were no accidents with the anti-freeze in the bubble towers! Insurance for the collection was always problematical, with the initial penguins costing as much as £1,600 on their arrival in the 1960s. In 1975 the final eleven penguins (two King penguins and nine Humboldt) were sold to Southampton Zoo, along with the terrapins. By 1990 only the flamingos remained and even they were eventually transferred to the Rhodes Bird Gardens, Somerset. With their removal the gardens were finally re-claimed by the employees of Birds Eye, freed from the tyranny of the penguin!

PÈRE DAVID'S DEER

Père David's deer actually owe their existence to gardens. These oddly shaped small deer are native to China, where their name '*sze pu shiang*' refers to their being made up of parts of various other animals, including the tail of a donkey and the hoofs of a cow. Human population growth having gradually reduced the swampy areas and open plains in which the deer lived, hunting finally drove the wild herds towards extinction. Fortunately a herd of the 'sze *pu shiang*' had been collected by the eighteenth century Emperor of China to decorate his park at Nan Hai-tsu, near Peking. Guarded by Tartar guards and surrounded by a seventy-two kilometre wall, the herd thrived in ideal conditions. Here they might have remained, known only to the few Chinese allowed to visit the park, and those who remembered the wild herds, if it were not for Père David. Père Armand David (1826–1900) was a French Jesuit missionary to China and keen (and inquisitive) naturalist. Strangers were forbidden to enter the park but Père David, having heard of the wonders kept within its walls, persuaded the tartar guards to allow him one look inside. On May 17 1865, at the exact moment that Père David was rewarded for his persuasive abilities, a herd of these strange deer wandered past his vantage point. Amazed by what he had seen, Père David was convinced that these were a species totally unknown to the European world. With all the persuasion a missionary can muster, Père David managed to 'liberate' two complete skins of the animals to send to Europe for identification. Confirmed in their uniqueness, although disappointed that his conviction that they were a new type of reindeer was wrong, he was honoured with the naming of the new species. Frantic diplomatic efforts resulted in three live deer being 'given' to the French by the Chinese Emperor, but by the time they arrived the deer were dead. Gifts to one European country have an unfortunate habit of having to be repeated to others, to avoid diplomatic 'incidents', and soon the Père David's deer were finding pastures (and gardens) new throughout Europe. Extinction loomed again for the Père David's deer, when the Emperor's private park was swept away by floods in 1895, and the very few deer that survived in China were killed during the Boxer Rebellion five years later. With only isolated individuals left scattered around Europe a decision was made to send all eighteen surviving deer to Woburn Park (Bedfordshire), to form a single breeding herd. Roaming free in the park the herd grew to some eighty animals, before the shortages of the First World War threatened their food supplies. Peace, followed by another war, saw fluctuating numbers, but eventually the parkland population reached over five hundred. In 1986 a decision was made to try and re-establish a Chinese population and twenty-two deer were sent to Peking, and released in the area of the old Imperial Park, where they were first discovered over 130 years ago. Woburn still contains several hundred Père David deer, estimated at a third of the world population of this still rare species.

PIG

Fyling Hall, North Yorkshire, contains what must be the most splendid pig house ever known. An inveterate traveller and graduate of the Grand Tour, the eccentric Squire Barry gave more care to the housing of his pair of Tamworth pigs than his pig keeper. Set within the parkland, the pigsty is an impressive stone and wood temple, with pillars, portico, fluted frieze, and tapering Egyptian windows. Drainpipe heads terminate in acanthus-leaf decoration in the style of the Corinthian column and

no expense was spared in decoration or comfort. The sty-cum-temple was recently purchased by the Landmark Trust and now houses holiday-makers, who can tactlessly rustle up a bacon sandwich in the newly installed kitchens.

PORCUPINE

Armed with a ready supply of offensive weapons and seemingly designed as the very antithesis of 'cuddly', the porcupine has rarely been kept as a house or garden pet (although even as I write these words I envisage a postbag of indignant letters from bands of hitherto unappreciated porcupine keepers!). However, as the Reverend Bingley pointed out in his *Animal Biography* the porcupine is predominantly inoffensive and generally harmless and although, as he adds, it rarely seems to show affection or attachment. Someone, somewhere was bound to choose it as a pet! That someone was Sir Ashton Lever (1729–1788) of Alkrington Hall, near Rochdale in Lancashire. Commencing his natural history studies with a collection of sea shells, a porcupine may not have seemed as studiously unaffectionate to Lever as it might have done had he been used to cuddly kittens. In fact the nearest Sir Ashton appears to have come to cuddly felines was a tame hunting leopard which he also acquired at the same period as the porcupine. The leopard, and a large Newfoundland dog would be let loose onto the lawns of Alkrington Hall to play together, although the description tends to suggest the 'play' was on the side of the leopard. As soon as they were let off the leashes, the leopard and dog would apparently pursue the poor porcupine who would first attempt to flee, and then bury his nose in a corner, pointing his spines towards his 'playmates'. Making a snorting noise and raising his spines, the porcupine relied on the foolishness of its aggressors – who would prick their noses and end up quarrelling amongst themselves, thus giving the porcupine an opportunity to escape. The leading of a porcupine on a leash was something also attempted by the keeper of the Tower of London, where one was kept in a menagerie. This example must have been particularly docile however as it would even let its keeper carry it around tucked under his arm, although as Bingley notes, to do this without sustaining wounds required considerable dexterity. Sir Ashton Lever obviously had some affinity with sharp points, as he founded the Royal Toxophilite Society, which, in case you are wondering, was responsible for the revival of interest in archery.

PURPLE SWAMPHEN

Also known as the African Swamphen, or the Sultana Bird, the purple swamphen is, as its name suggests, a purplish bird which prefers wet areas. According to the Roman author, Pliny the Elder, these birds were popular with Roman nobility, who would use them to decorate their villa gardens. Certainly they would bring a riot of colour! The body colouring is purple and blue, the bill is red, and the legs and feet orange-red. As the Purple Swamphen walks, it flicks its tail up and down, revealing its white undertail. The call is also distinctive: a loud, penetrating 'kee-ow' (described by some authorities as 'a raucous high-pitched skreech'), as well as some softer clucking between members of a group while feeding. Regarded as noble birds, they were the only birds that the Romans did not eat (unlike their other garden 'pets' the dormouse and the edible snail!). The size of a chicken, the swamphen added colour and movement to the otherwise formal gardens.

QUAGGA

Arriving to ornament the king's gardens of Versailles just five years in advance of the French Revolution, the quagga may have felt the auguries for its survival were not good. It was however to be one of the longer lasting members of the king's collections, surviving the turmoil of 1789 when so many others were swept away. This 'stripped horse' was to become one of the founding specimens of the small zoo at the *Jardin des Plantes*, set up with revolutionary zeal from animals taken from Versailles by Bernardin de Saint-Pierre.

Bernardin was said to be an arch-romantic and he would have surely appreciated the irony of such a solitary survivor representing a species that would become extinct only a hundred years later. Of the quagga that took revolution in its stride, only the skin now remains, housed in the extinct animals hall of the *Muséum National d'Histoire Naturelle*.

QUAGGA AND QUAGGONK

Owston Park, Doncaster sounds as though it should contain, if anything, owls, albeit without the 'l'. But in the 1820s it was instead home to a large herd of quagga, perhaps the largest ever group in Europe. Philip Davies-Cooke, the owner of Owston at the time, also owned estates in Wales and South Africa, and it was from South Africa that he had his quagga imported. Living on the ancestral acres, the herd were an attractive stripy alternative to the more usual deer. Visually, although not literally, a cross between a zebra and a small horse, the quaggas proved surprisingly docile and were sufficiently tamed to be useful as well as decorative. A female of the herd was trained to draw a small cart, in which Philip and Lady Helen Davies-Cooke would tour the estate. Whether there were also zebra, or whether there was an understandable stripy confusion, a local blacksmith claimed to still be shoeing zebra to perform this task into the twentieth century. Even more confusingly, Davies-Cooke experimented with cross-breeding between a quagga and a donkey, which produced a Quaggonk, although sadly the mother and sole offspring died.

RABBIT

The Renaissance gardens of the Villa Barbarigo in the Italian Veneto, are an allegory of man's progress towards his own perfectibility or salvation. Beginning at the Temple of Diana, the gardens progress across the Valle de St Eusebio (giving the site its alternative name of Valsanzibio), to Diana's Bath, the Rainbow Fountain, the Maze of Life, the Hermitage of St Eusebio, and on to a monumental Statue of Time. Time himself overlooks the Rabbit Island, representing Immanence, and from there one progresses towards the Fountain of Revelation. The rabbit's role in this splendid progression was to demonstrate, somewhat literally, the overcoming of mortality and the bounds of time by the procreation and continuation of life through succeeding generations. Confined to an island in the gardens, in case animal procreation otherwise overcame vegetative growth and the Maze of Life was no more, the rabbits were housed in a magnificent stone warren. This up-market rabbitry was surrounded by railings and a moat (one cannot be too careful with rabbits!) and had the addition of a central ironwork aviary. Here, if the paintings of the early eighteenth century artist Rossetti, are to be believed, they flourished and bred in a very satisfactory allegorical manner.

RABBIT II

No book on pets and gardens could possibly fail to include those most famous of rabbits, Benjamin Bunny and Peter Rabbit. In fact the rabbits whom these much-loved creations of Beatrix Potter were based on were Benjamin Bouncer and a real-life Peter. Living throughout her childhood in the centre of London, most of Beatrix's pets were kept secure in her third floor nursery in Kensington where she spent most of her days well into adulthood. Here lived most of the animals that were later destined to appear in her books: a green frog named Punch; two lizards, Toby and Judy; some water newts; Sally, a ring-necked snake; minnows; a dormouse named Xarifa; two house mice, Hunca Munca and Thomas Thumb, whom the butler had caught in the kitchen; birds; bats; a family of snails; guinea pigs; and a hedgehog named Mrs. Tiggy-Winkle. Benjamin Bouncer, probably a cross with a jack-hare rather than a pure bred rabbit, and Peter, were allowed not only the house but also the delights of the outside world. Taken regularly for walks in the garden, they would be harnessed and allowed to explore on a long lead. When summer came and the Potter family decamped to their Lake District summer home Benjamin, and later Peter, would accompany them. Benjamin was originally purchased from a London birdshop in 1885, when Beatrix was nineteen years old. He was smuggled into the house in a paper bag, becoming the model for many of her illustrations and the inspiration for her Christmas cards to the family in 1889. On the back of a photograph of Benjamin Beatrix wrote "'This is the original 'Benjamin Bunny'. Benjamin was extremely fond

of hot buttered toast, he used to hurry into the drawing room when he heard the tea-bell!'' When Beatrix's first greetings cards portraying Benjamin were accepted by a publisher she rewarded him with a cupful of help seeds, the consequence being that he was 'partially intoxicated and wholly unmanageable' the next morning when she wanted to draw him. It was Benjamin's gourmet tendencies which proved the end of him, as he died from a surfeit of peppermints, having lived in luxury for nine years. Peter Piper was a Belgian buck rabbit 'bought at a very tender age' from a shop in the Uxbridge Rd, London. Beatrix wrote in a letter to a child, 'Peter used to lie before the fire on the hearth-rug like a cat. He was clever at learning tricks, he used to jump through a hoop, and ring a bell, and play the tambourine. I saw him once trying to play the tambourine on a straw hat!' Peter was destined to have a long and happy life, sharing the house and garden walks for over ten years, until his demise in 1901, by which time Beatrix was thirty-five. In 1891 Rupert Potter took a wonderful photograph of Benjamin Bouncer in his harness and lead, being walked in the gaterden by Beatrix. The photograph survived in the archives of the V&A Museum, London. Neither would have realised that they were posing for generations of fans to come, nor that rabbit harnesses and leads would one day be common items for sale in pet shops.

RACCOON

Rebecca the raccoon is probably the most famous raccoon in American history and the only one to have lived at the White House. One of many different types of animals sent to President Coolidge and his First Lady, Grace Coolidge, the others including wombats, bears, a hippopotamus and a pair of lion cubs (called Tax Reduction and Budget Bureau), the raccoon was sent from Peru, Mississippi, and was initially destined for the Thanksgiving Dinner. On arrival the raccoon was found to be too tame to sauté and instead a house was made for her in one of the tall trees in the grounds of the presidential palace, with a wire fence built around it for protection. President Coolidge announced her arrival at a press conference where he reported that she was at home in the 'south lot' 'He' (for some reason Coolidge insisted on calling the raccoon 'he'), 'seems to be enjoying himself very much ... I don't think he is quite grown yet. He is very playful, very interesting, and seems very well trained and well behaved'. At that stage a name had not been chosen and the press were asked to run a competition for one. Although one feels that the president put entries at a disadvantage by indicating the wrong sex for the animal. Rebecca was kept outside either in her 'tree enclosure' or on a chain in the grounds, to prevent her escaping. However she was eventually allowed to come indoors as well, and had to be carefully watched. She was a mischievous, inquisitive soul who enjoyed nothing better than being placed in a bathtub with a little water in it and given a cake of soap with which to play. In this fashion she would amuse herself for an hour or more. Rebecca would take her meals either on the tiled floor of her mistress' bathroom or in the house in the garden. While most Americans of the time were dining on a relatively simple diet, Rebecca seemed a veritable gourmet with green shrimp, chicken, persimmon, eggs (a particular favourite), and cream. On 18 April 1927 the First Lady showed Rebecca off at the White House Easter Egg Roll where she was photographed by the presidential press pack. Rebecca escaped from the grounds on a few occassions, but each time was recaptured. On 4 July 1927, *Time Magazine* reported 'Rebecca Raccoon got out of her stable again, climbed a high tree. The White House staff formed a posse, located Rebecca, but could not induce her to come down. Mrs. Coolidge coaxed, President Coolidge whistled, Rebecca remained intransigent. Dispatches added that another raccoon had been prowling about the State Lodge since Rebecca's arrival, adding sex appeal to reports of Rebecca's escapade. The Coolidges, fearing she would be run over in the street on one last jaunt, eventually turned her over to the Rock Creek Zoo for her own safety. Concerned for her long term happiness they prevailed upon zoo officials to secure some companionship for her, arriving in the form of a male raccoon dubbed Reuben. The match-making unfortunately failed as Reuben escaped from the zoo, leaving Rebecca to live a solitary life.

RAT

Many are the admonitory signs that can be found in public parks. No ball games, no walking on the grass, no feeding of the ducks, no fishing, no cycling, no fun. But Peckham Rye Park boasted one of the most unusual: 'Don't feed the rats'. Deprived presumably of the more normal pet, the children of Peckham in the early twentieth century had taken to bring-

ing small bags of food to these chubby vermin. As the *Daily Chronicle* of the period recorded 'The little park ... is one of the prettiest in London, and the rats have made it also one of the most popular. You can find peacocks and pigeons in the park. But if you discover a little group of children with paper bags in their hands, you may take it for granted that they are there not to feed the birds but the rats.'

RAVEN

Occasionally the stories told of the antics of animals kept in gardens are such that one wonders whether the animal was kept on purpose to taunt a much disliked gardener. One such is the story related in the Victorian periodical, the *New Monthly Magazine* and repeated in *The Parlour Menagerie*. The correspondent in this case had acquired a pet raven that was allowed the freedom of house and garden. Describing the bird as being 'the most mischievous and amusing creature he ever met with' the owner related a story to support this assertion. 'The raven', he wrote, 'would get into the flower garden, go to the beds where the gardener had sowed a great variety of seeds with sticks in the ground with labels, and then he would amuse himself with pulling up every stick and laying them in heaps of ten or twelve on the path. This used to irritate the old gardener very much, who would drive him away. The raven knew that he ought not to do it or he would not have done it. He would soon return to his mischief, and when the gardener again chased him (the old man could not run very fast), the raven would just keep clear of the rake or the hoe in his hand, dancing before him and singing, as plain as a raven might do, 'tol de rol, tol de rol'. Tame ravens (and indeed magpies, rooks and crows) were relatively common in the nineteenth century, one also being kept by the Earl of Aylesbury who taught it to talk, to the considerable surprise of those whom it met in its rambles around his Wiltshire country seat. The Earl's raven fortunately preferred to taunt the cattle in his park with his cheery 'Hallos', leaving his gardener unmolested.

RED DEER

Red deer are most usually seen in large herds, gracing magnificent English parkland but at Chatsworth, Derbyshire, the quiet of the evening would see a tame red deer hind called Sarah promenading the rose garden. Fond of ginger biscuits and Polo mints, Sarah would creep up on people noiselessly, startling them with a sudden awareness of breathing and a friendly presence.

RHINOCEROS

Although this collection of garden animals has largely eschewed the zoological collection and public menageries, an exception must surely be made for the tame rhinoceros that was allowed to wander freely in the grounds of the Belle Vue Zoological Gardens, Manchester. Descended perhaps from the eighteenth century rhinoceroses that were kept as 'docile pets' by Javanese nobleman, this particular example would wander through the gardens, munching the vegetation and wallowing in the lake. So leisurely were its wallows that it had to be actually chased out of the mud when visitors wished to see it. A homely touch was apparently added to the scene by the addition of the family home of Belle Vue's proprietor within the gardens, and the presence of their washing line on view to visitor and rhinoceros alike. The laundry unfortunately proved a temptation to even the most domesticated of rhinoceros, and Mrs Jennison's laundry was subjected to the ruminant chewings of a homesick rhino. Developed from Tea Gardens in the 1830s, the Belle Vue gardens covered some 13 acres by the 1830s, so at the time of the rhino's residence there was plenty of scope for a wander and a wallow, not to mention the odd nibble on linen. The creature ended its days by being exhibited in the Manchester Museum where its skull still remains, recently being re-discovered and claimed as the earliest example of a Javanese Rhinoceros in the country. Also located in the Manchester Museum basement, alongside the skull, used to be an ancient rolled up rhino hide soaking in a large barrel of brine. Although not positively recorded as being from the same animal, decades of soaking seem an ironically suitable fate for an animal fond of consuming drying laundry.

ROOK

In the days when eating habits were somewhat more adventurous, or at least undiscriminating, rooks were often featured on menus, along with the rather better known 'four and twenty' blackbirds. Rookeries were then seen as an advantageous aspect of a garden, and were often listed in sales catalogues by estate agents bent on extolling every virtue of a house and its grounds. Occasionally birds that fell out of these rookeries, or indeed 'wild' rookeries, would be taken in and domesticated. Such was the case with Jack, the tame rook that belonged to Edward Coward in the early 1920s, and whom Edward eloquently described in *The Spectator* magazine. Jack had been, literally, a 'drop out' from the rookery on Edward's land, but had been fortunate enough not only to have a soft landing, but also a soft-hearted finder. Initially fed and housed in a cage, as soon as he was old enough Jack was allowed to roost in a silver birch tree in the garden, from where he would admire the domestic activities of the garden. A terror to the dogs sleeping on the lawn, Jack would fly down and give them a hard dig with his beak, rapidly returning to his perch on the gate or the birch tree, where he was inaccessible to the no-longer sleeping dogs. In common with other birds such as crows and jackdaws, Jack was also fascinated with small labels, shiny objects and small seedlings, with the inevitable result of frustration and confusion in the seed beds. These acts of vandalism were apparently tolerated by Edward's mother (the aggrieved and injured gardener in this case) on account of Jack being otherwise so entertaining; When Jack started to remove the wallpaper from the interior house-walls a limit had been overstepped, and Jack was sent to live in a stables, from whence he escaped back into the wild rookery in disgust. His call was heard once or twice from the rookery and the Cowards mourned for their 'intelligent, mischievous and amusing pet'. The publication of the history of Jack in *The Spectator* was hotly followed by letters claiming the superiority of an assortment of jackdaws and crows, all of whom appear to have had the same addiction to puling up labels and seedlings!

SCARLET IBIS

Many a gardener has been watched attentively by the cheerful red-breasted robin, alert for the insects and worms disturbed by the gardener's activities. The gardener of M. Delaborde, French naturalist and correspondent with the Zoological Society was pursued by something rather more substantial, and even more colourful. M. Delaborde kept a Scarlet Ibis for a pet, admiring greatly its scarlet plumage and its statuesque figure. He fed the bird on a diet of bread, raw or cooked meat and fish, but noted that it supplemented that diet by following his gardener around the grounds in pursuit of earthworms disturbed in his labours. At night it would retire to roost on the highest perch of the poultry house, flying abroad again the next morning in its horticultural searches.

SHEEP

The Presidential White House is not normally associated with either rurality or money-saving schemes. However during the war and depression years of 1913 to 1921 President Woodrow Wilson attempted to cut ground-keeping costs by 'employing' sheep to trim the lawns to a fine downland finish. In addition to the savings on grass cutting machines, the sheep's wool was collected, and a photograph survives of a mountain of this further contribution to the war effort. Included in the patriotic flock was the infamous 'Old Ike' a ram with an addiction to tobacco chewing. In 2002 the White House Christmas decorations took the theme of 'Presidential Pets' and included three sheep on the mantelpiece, a rather wild-eyed individual might have represented Old Ike.

SNAIL

Along with dormice, the edible snail (*Locus cochlaeriis*) was much prized by the Romans and as early as the first century BC small moated 'rockeries' were being constructed in shady garden corners for the keeping of these tasty invertebrates. This Roman habit was repeated in eighteenth century England at the royal gardens of Richmond Palace and Kensington where combined snaileries and tortoise enclosures were constructed under the instruction of George I (monarch 1714-27). Constructed by the Office of Works the snailery consisted of a shallow trough in the garden, lined with lead with a small fence dividing it from the tortoise enclosure. The fence was necessary not because of unexpectedly carnivorous tortoises but because the enclosure contained a water tank three feet deep that would have proved hazardous for the snails. Thus the two species were kept separate, probably only meeting on the dinner plate. In 1727 a young tiger, an old tiger and a civet cat were also recorded at the palace gardens, a remnant of an earlier menagerie, but it is the snailery which stirs the imagination.

SNAKE

Walter Ambrose Heath Harding M.A. appeared from his biographical entry in Pike's *East Anglia*, to be a perfectly normal Edwardian gentleman. Son of Colonel Thomas Harding, educated at Cheltenham and Peterhouse, his interests included travel, sketching, skating and supporting the Conservative cause. A member of the Constitutional Club and the Linnean Society he lunched at St James'. An additional comment however shed a different light on the man who owned Histon Manor, Cambridgeshire. He had, it said 'a small collection of live wild animals' and had published observations on reptiles. A 1927 Sales Catalogue for the house confirms the presence, between the house and the kitchen gardens, of a 'menagerie building, 38x15ft, with a 'tortoise' boiler (in this instance the make of boiler rather than its purpose!). The 'menagerie' was in fact a snake and reptile pit, containing a variety of exotic warmth loving snakes. Brick built, with a sunken floor and a thatched roof, the snake house presented a pleasingly rustic, or perhaps African, appearance probably adapted from existing hot-houses. Anticipating few prospective buyers with a need for a snake-house the estate agents catalogue hastily suggested that it might be adapted to make an ideal 'double garage'. This adaptation was never made and the snake-house remained, an exotic outpost in a small Cambridgeshire village.

SPARROW

The glorious swirling colours of Monet's impressionist paintings were inspired by the artist's own gardens at Giverney, France. Nearest the house a kaleidoscope of colours were mixed and matched to make a palette, whilst in the water lily garden the dappled reflections created a serenity of clouds and water. Monet however was not content with the colours, but wanted 'to paint as a bird sings'. Perhaps to this end he had enclosures created in the gardens for a colourful and vocal array of golden pheasants, black ducks and white hens. He also nursed wounded birds, including a one-legged sparrow which for over three years took breadcrumbs from the table. However cheerful, the chirruping sparrow is not really a tune which brings to mind the glory of Monet's paintings, although less discordant than the peacocks which he also kept.

SQUIRREL

A cloudless Edwardian afternoon, the idyllic fir forests above Lake Geneva, a carpet of gentians and, of course, a picnic – the scene was set for the entry of Romulus the squirrel. A victim of the insatiable appetite for collecting nesting birds, the squirrel was found in what had been presumed to be a magpie's nest. However reprehensible its removal might seen today, the collectors of this little bundle, still blind and hairless, were determined to take care of it once they had found it. Taking it to the nearest café they ordered a *café au lait* for it, which it apparently gulped down (an expensive habit!). They then offered it to the cat at their Swiss pension, not as an overfed comestible, but rather in the hope that she would add it to her current nurslings. Rather unbelievably she did so, perhaps having mislaid one of her own co-incidentally. The squirrel grew rapidly, becoming a handsome bushy-tailed creature with large black eyes. In the cat's eyes it was a favourite, if somewhat unexpectedly troublesome. One day the cat was spied sitting alone anxiously by the open window, awaiting the return of her 'kitten' from its new playground on the roof of the house. A few weeks later she led her offspring out into the garden, with the air of a matron leading a *débutante*, and abandoned him there. The squirrel was in his element, racing around the shrubs and trees, and eventually making his home in the tall Tulip Tree close to the house. Extraordinarily tame he enlivened the days of his original (undeserving) 'finders' by joining them in their garden tea parties, and searching their pockets for biscuits. First thing in the mornings he would leap from the tree tops through the house windows and sit on the beds, begging for nuts and treats that they kept in their pillows for him. Ann Wood (who sent his story to *The Spectator* in the 1920s) named him Romulus as he had been brought up by a different species of animal, and he would come leaping to the call of 'Rom, Rom' in search of treats. After spending a merry summer in the gardens he suddenly left in the November, perhaps off to found his own family. Many of the titbits which he had extracted from the family were found later in a secret larder, a hollow tree in the garden, biscuits all gone soft. After Mary Woods and her family also left, to return to England, their Swiss landlady doubtless found more soggy biscuits in their bed linen and in her neat Swiss window boxes.

SWAN

The chateau and gardens of Malmaison are famed throughout the world as the one time home of Josephine, fanati-
cal rose lover, amateur naturalist, and wife of Napoleon
Bonaparte. Originating from Martinique, Marie Joseph
Rose de Tascher left her tropical homeland at the age of
fifteen as bride to Alexandre de Beauharnais. Widowed in
1794, courtesy of the guillotine, two years later a trans-
formed Josephine married the man who was to become
the most powerful in all of Europe. Although officially
based at the Tulleries, with its extensive formal gardens,
Josephine longed for the rural life (at least in theory)
and purchased the chateau of Malmaison, eight miles to
the west of Paris as a retreat for herself and children.
Childhood memories of the exotic plants and animals
of Martinique prompted Josephine to create a garden at
Malmaison which would be 'the most beautiful and curious
in Europe'. A garden in which the paradise of 'equality' met
the paradise of Eden and all was harmony, most especially
as the fiercer animals were banished to the less elysian
fields of the *Muséum national d'Histoire naturelle*. As Marie
Antoinette had done before her at Versailles, Josephine
would revert at Malmaison to the rural delights although
unlike Marie Antoinette's home grown *ferme ornée*, the
sheep at Malmaison were from Asia and the swans from
Australia. Black swans had first been described in Europe
by travellers to the new found continent in 1697, on the
west coast river now known (predictably) as Swan River.
Totally black, apart from their white quill feather and their
red beak, the birds were to become a lasting emblem

of Josephine's garden. Collected by a French expedition sailing in *Le Naturaliste* and *Le Géographe*, a pair of swans, along with other exotic pants and animals, was brought to Malmaison to live free amongst the trees and flowers that echoed their native lands. How they were captured is unknown as it was noted by the London Zoological Society that this species of bird was 'said to be extremely shy, so as to render it difficult to approach within gunshot of them'. Very wisely! Arriving at Malmaison however they must have lost their natural reticence, as in a triumph for her reputation as a naturalist, Josephine managed to establish the first ever breeding pair of black swans in Europe. The original pair that had arrived in 1803 produced over fifty cygnets, and were the highlight of Malmaison, especially after the sad demise of many of the kangaroos. Black swans became a fashion motif of the Empire, joining Empire furnishings and Empire clocks as the essential for every fashionable house and garden. Josephine herself had swan motifs (in black and white) throughout the furnishings at Malmaison, appearing on carpets, wall friezes and even as part of armchairs. Ironically just as the black swans were forming their monogamous, and fruitful, romantic attachments, Josephine's own marriage was failing apart. Failing to provide an heir, she was increasingly sidelined and, in 1809, Napoleon divorced her, before he himself became an exile in 1814. The black swans of Malmaison finally outlived them both, their descendants conquering those parts of Europe that Napoleon himself never reached.

SWAN II

To dance the role of the Dying Swan is one of ballet's most coveted parts, and following its creation by Fokine in 1905 it has become associated with some of the world's most famous ballet dancers. Anna Pavlova, prima ballerina of the Imperial Ballet at St Petersburg, was one of these and to celebrate the success of the part an admirer presented Pavlova with a pair of mute swans that she housed in her spectacular garden at Ivy House, in Golders Green, London. Jack, and his mate, rather appropriately arrived at Ivy House soon after Anna had had the lake enlarged to house her varied collection, inspired as she was by the flight of birds. Jack, like many male swans, was a splendid and large bird, but rather unapproachable and with a distinct temper. On her return to Britain in 1918 Pavlova was approached by a swan expert who offered to tame Jack, with astounding results. Jack became quite docile, and would follow Pavlova around the garden. Pavlova would take him on her knees and twine his neck around hers in a pose of utmost beauty; ballerina and swan entwined in curves of harmony. Jack took all this without the slightest protest and the resulting pose was captured on camera. When not posing for the cameras Jack managed to raise a family and, at his death at the age of fifteen, he was succeeded by his son, also Jack. Anna Pavlova died before reaching fifty, having exhausted herself with her world tours and performances and Jack II outlived his mistress. The astounding double portrait photograph may be seen in the National Portrait Gallery, London, giving substance to the legend of Zeus seducing Leda whilst in the guise of a swan.

TERRAPIN

Long before 'Ninja Turtles' led to an unfortunate outbreak of terrapins being flushed into the waste system
(alive or dead) they were of fascination for visitors to
Wotton House, Surrey. Originally the home of the diarist
John Evelyn, who kept bees in glass hives, the terrapins
were introduced to Wotton by his nineteenth century
descendants. Both George Evelyn and his son, William
John Evelyn, were extremely fond of animals, keeping
zebra, wild swine and zebu at Wotton, and extended this
love to aquatic mammals. The terrapin house, probably
built in c1820–1830, was constructed in the style of a
classical temple with an Ionic pillared portico of four bays,
floors of black and white marble, niches for classical statu-
ary and large upper windows to allow light to stream into
the pools below. The detail was described by Nikolaus
Pevsner in his series *The Buildings of England*, as 'delicate;
the idea reminiscent of a Chinese Tea House' adding that
the building is 'unique'. A wooden pedimented 'summerhouse' allowed visitors to watch the terrapins playing in
the pools below, pools which were kept clean by the
constant flow of water from one of the tributaries of
the River Tillingbourne. What exact species (or indeed
genus) of amphibians were kept in this classical paradise
is not known. The Red-eared terrapin has been suggested
as most possible from the description of the facilities,
but land tortoises were considerably more common and
could have included Greek, Hermann's or Spur-Thighed
tortoise or the more aquatic yellow-spotted European
Pond Tortoise. This unusual taste in garden pets by John

Evelyn's descendant was echoed in the other garden animals, which included chameleons, and a vulture. The present owners do not share such tastes and the terrapin (or tortoise) temple has fallen into disrepair.

TOAD

Even before the advent of the ecological 'wildlife' garden, toads apparently fetched a high price from those anxious to establish a colony. Their insect eating activities made them invaluable in the garden and the cucumber frame, or as the America humorist Mr Dudley Warner said, 'no melon patch is complete without a toad'. Professional florists would import them in hundreds onto their premises, and the country was scoured by small children wanting to make some pocket money. The Reverend Wood felt that the gardening duties of the toad had served to eclipse his worth as an affectionate pet, for 'although by no means a creature famous for intelligence, if it be kindly treated, [the toad] soon comes to know its owner, and even to evince some sort of affection for him.'. This affection apparently took the form of coming to the owners call, sitting on his hand, and taking flies direct from his fingers; licking being (thankfully) beyond the affectionate nature of the toad. Every garden pet has its weakness and that of the toad was its lack of discrimination between different insects and grubs. Kept in the garden (and house) to dispose of cockroaches, flies and aphids they also partook of the rather more attractive glow-worms and butterflies. The Reverend Wood collected his own toads on a warm April day, and brought all thirty-six home on the railway, a noisy experience as the toads chose to croak all the way home. He installed them in a small ornamental fernery, where he provided them with small caves and tiny grottoes. Allowed to 'run' loose amongst the ferns they provided animation, and if the Rev. Wood is to be believed, affection. One unfortunate evening the Reverend decided to expand his fernery collection to include between fifty and sixty glow-worms, which took him some considerable time to collect. These were let loose to cast their green light amongst the shadows of the fronds, and very beautiful they apparently looked. By the morning only half-a-dozen of the shining insects survived, and by the following day none at all. All had fallen foul of the long and rapid tongue of the pet toads. Resigned to the loss of his glow-worms the reverend took a Christian viewpoint stating that: 'After all, the toad cannot be expected to discriminate between the insects which we admire and those which we consider injurious. And in every other way he can be most recommended as a pet'. The Rev. Wood also kept frogs in his fernery, which in turn fell foul of a tame hedgehog.

TORTOISE

The first recorded tortoise keeper in England was the ecclesiast William Laud (1573–1645) who kept his in the garden of Fulham Palace. The tortoise (most probably a Spur-thighed tortoise) reputedly lived an astounding 128 years before being accidentally killed by an under-gardener in 1753 – long after the death of Laud. Indeed ecclesiastics appear to have an empathy with these Methusalahs of the animal world as the Bishops of Peterborough (several of them) also kept a tortoise in the gardens of their Bishop's palace. Supposedly born in *c*.1600 the almost immortal tortoise outlived seven Bishops to die only in 1821. The animal was recorded as eating a diet of endive, green peas, and leeks, but positively rejecting asparagus, parsley and spinach. In the early part of the season its favourite food was the flower of the dandelion, of which it would eat twenty at one sitting (do tortoises 'sit'?). It was also partial to the pulp of an orange. Later in the season the admirably productive Bishop's garden would furnish the tortoise with currants, raspberries, pears, plums, apples, peaches, nectarines, strawberries and gooseberries – of which it would eat a pint for a single meal. So enamoured was it of gooseberries that it would watch the gardener attentively and follow him if he moved towards the gooseberry bushes to harvest the fruits. Weighing in at a massive thirteen pounds and a half, unsurprisingly this gourmet tortoise turned his nose up at the humble carrot or turnip. Retrospective identification of the exact species of this animal is fraught with difficulties as there is no description of its shell, his diet having been of more fascination to the Bishops. There is though a theory that he may have been a very obese Marginated tortoise, which seems to fit with the evidence of his eating habits. Unlike Timothy the Selborne tortoise, the shell was never kept and the opportunities for verification were lost. Given the astounding (if not miraculous) age the reptile supposedly reached it is a great shame that he was not given immortality in a museum, although a religious burial might have been more appropriate.

TORTOISE II

The seventeenth century diarist and gardener, John Evelyn, also kept a tortoise. He records its unfortunate death in the extremely harsh winter of 1683 in his garden at Sayes Court.

TORTOISE III

Timothy, the tortoise who inhabited the Gilbert White's garden at Selborne led a long, and unusually well documented, life. Famous for his *Natural History of Selborne* published in 1788, the Reverend White kept a detailed journal of the daily happenings in his garden and the surrounding landscape from 1768 until his death in 1793. The journal recorded the comings and goings of birds, flowering of garden and wild plants, ripening of fruits and of course the seasonal perambulations in the life of the tortoise, Timothy, bequeathed to him by his aunt, Mrs Snooke. Timothy had been purchased by Mrs Snooke in Chichester in 1740, when she had seen the tortoise being sold by a sailor for half a crown. He lived in the shelter of her walled garden in Sussex for the next thirty years, until Mrs Snooke's death in 1770 when he was 'left' to Gilbert. Dug out of his winter dormitory to be transported to his new home in Selborne Timothy was awake enough to express his resentment at this treatment by hissing. He was carefully packed in a box with earth for the eighty mile journey to his new home by post-chaise. Timothy lived freely in the garden at Selborne rambling amongst the 'umbrageous forests of the asparagus-beds', sunning himself beneath the laurel hedge, and just occasionally being tempted beyond the garden limits. Weighing 'six pounds three quarters, two ounces and a half' in 1777 he had not put on any weight by the end of the following summer despite a large a varied diet including devouring kidney beans and cucumbers 'in a most voracious manner'. Fortunately for Timothy, Gilbert White was a prodigious cucumber grower, recording the cutting of 550 cucumbers in just two weeks in the September of 1790. Enough to keep the most voracious tortoise happy. Life in the Selborne garden had its dangers, and in 1782 an unusually hard rainstorm found Timothy 'almost flooded in his hybernaculum amidst the laurel-hedge; and might have been drowned, had not his friend Thomas come to his assistance & taken him away'. November was the usual month which saw Timothy churning up the earth to bury himself in his hybernaculum against the coming cold months, although in the December of 1774, after a month's burial, he came forth and 'wandered around the garden in a disconsolate state' due to the mild weather. His brief reappearance in March of the following year was rather startlingly accompanied by the journal note 'Earth-worms lie about and copulate'. In the heady June of 1787, Timothy's amorous pursuits led him 'beyond the bounds of his usual gravity at this season' and he went missing for two days in pursuit of love; being found at last near the upper malt house. The chilly August of the same year found amour replaced by slumber as Timothy started to become sluggish and refuse food in preparation for hibernation. Timothy was not alone in attracting the attentions of the Rev. Gilbert White, who also noted the re-emergence of Mr Loveday's tortoise whilst on a trip to Reading. Timothy outlived his owner by one year, dying in 1794. In 1853 his carapace was presented to the Museum of Natural History, where it still resides, allowing the classification of *Testudo whiteii*. Timothy was in fact a female.

TREE FROG

Lord Egerton of Tatton Park used the Paxton-designed fernery there to keep his collection of tree frogs and snakes. Allowed to roam free and bask on the leaves of the tropical plantings, the collection specialised in the more exotic varieties. With their unpleasant habits of spitting venom at passers-by they deterred many a visitor to the esteemed fern collection. When Sam Youd, the current head gardener, arrived in the 1970s there were still people who recalled the tree frogs and their less than sociable behaviour, alongside their equally objectionable companions, South African snakes. The newly restored fernery has dispensed with such highlights.

TURKEY

Henrietta, Lady Luxborough had a small aviary in her gardens at Barrells Hall, which contained canaries, guinea-fowl and 'turkies'. The turkeys were given space to roam and their aesthetic sensibilities catered for by a fountain placed within their aviary, which also formed an attractive garden feature. The turkeys might have preferred more security to aesthetics however, as one night twenty 'plum turkeys' were taken by a raiding pole-cat, with a further eight disappearing the following afternoon. The aviary could be admired from Lady Luxborough library which was perhaps unfortunate for the few turkeys that escaped the attentions of the pole-cat as Henrietta was inspired to make her writing quills from their long wing feathers. Doubtless serviceable enough for the actual writing, she felt that they sadly failed to impart wit to her letters, an attribute which her correspondent the landscape gardener William Shenstone claims he gained from his goose feather. 'If my turkeys carried so much wit in their quills [as your goose], they should not live to morning' she wrote to him in December of 1748. The loss of wit was perhaps compensated for by their ornamental effect in her garden.

TURKEY II

President Abraham Lincoln, 16th President of the USA, was known equally for his love for his family and his animals. He allowed his sons, Tad and Willie, to keep as many pets as they wished. The result was a menagerie that included rabbits, turkeys, horses, and even two goats, Nanny and Nanko. One special animal in the Lincoln White House was Jack the turkey. Jack was originally scheduled to appear on the Lincoln's dinner menu, but Tad became fond of the bird during its 'fattening up' and pleaded with his father to spare Jack's life, President Lincoln relented, and Jack became part of the Presidential household. On Election Day 1864, while the Civil War raged close to Washington, D.C., a special booth was placed on the White House grounds so that soldiers serving nearby could vote. President Lincoln, his private secretary Noah Brooks, and Tad were watching from an upstairs window when they saw Jack strut out among the voters. 'Why is your turkey at the polls? Does he vote?' Lincoln asked his son. 'No,' Tad answered, 'he's not of age yet'.

WALLABY

A short article in the *Daily News* of 3 August 1900 considered the word 'paradise'. Paradise, the writer claimed, was a term for an area where foreign birds and animals have been successfully acclimatised and live in wild conditions in English parks and gardens. Of the three examples it gave of 'paradise' (Haggerstone Castle, Woburn and Leonardslee) the writer in the *Daily News* proposed Leonardslee Gardens, Sussex, as the most successful. Here, in the gentle Sussex landscape, lived prairie dogs, mouflon sheep, Patagonian cavie, and, most notably, wallabies. A hundred years on, the mouflon and prairie dogs have disappeared, but the wallabies still charm the visitors with their antics. The first ornamental plantings at Leonardslee date back to the early 1800s, but it was Sir Edmund Loder who created much of the present garden from 1899 onwards, and imported the herd of wallabies. Widely travelled, Sir Edmund Loder (1849–1920) was a naturalist with a penchant for exotic plants from the Himalayas and China, as well as exotic animals. Much of his 'collecting' was in the typical Victorian method of sudden death and Loder had a fine selection of heads of all types of deer, including the rare Loder's gazelle named after him. Returning to settle at the family home, he brought not only many exotic deer and gazelle but also wallabies (with their heads). To make the mouflon and wallabies feel 'at home' an enclosure of artificial rocks was created within the Leonardslee gardens by James Pulham, using the famous Pulhamite 'rockwork' of cement over rubble. A large mound, topped by a ring of conifers was created, with caves set into it to provide breeding pens away from the early visitors. Paths leading up the mound were favoured by the mouflon, but not the wallabies, who preferred to sit with their back to the warm stonework, sunning their tummies. Naturalised to the English weather they now hop and graze on the grassy swards, below amongst the colourful camellias and rhododendrons many of which were also introduced into the country by Sir Edmund Loder. It is not known at what date the famous albino wallabies made an appearance, but now several of these unusual looking animals also decorate the gardens. Robin Loder, present head of the family, comments that the wallabies are the most efficient of ground management operatives, working seven days a week, fifty-two weeks a year to maintain rough grassy banks and asking no pay, petrol or pension rights whilst attracting visitors who watch them 'work'. They live semi-wild and, unlike sheep, do not spoil the carefully grazed sward by leaving walking trails, as they graze independently rather than in herds. The soft pads on the bottoms of their feet cause no damage to the wildflower population, and their small droppings conveniently fertilise the ground as they mow. As well as its wallabies, Leonardslee is also still famous for its rhododendrons, most famously the hybrid *Rhododendron Loderi* of which there are several varieties (*R. loderi* 'King George', *R. loderi* Pretty Polly' etc), as well as the spectacular *Rhododendron* 'Loders White', which rather pleasingly complements the pure white of the albino wallabies.

WALLABY II

By 1927 Scottish country houses and gardens were seemingly about to be overrun by wallabies. R. Scott Miller, writing in the Amateur Menagerie Club Yearbook recalled seeing the first at The Marquis of Bute's home on the island of Bute over thirty years before, (along with a colony of beavers) whilst Miller himself had been keeping them on the lawns outside his house for 13 years, with great success. His original pair had been obtained from Sir Edmund Loder of Leonardslee (see entry above). The wallabies bred happily in Miller's garden and grounds, having a young one every one or two years and his small group of four provided him with ample opportunity for observing their life cycle. Certainly he found them entertaining and endearing, describing the young in pouch as having the air of a bleary eyed Whippet puppy. They lived mainly on grass with some broken biscuits and roots and were provided with a wooden shed in which to shelter from the worst of the weather in Scotland, although he observed that they grew thicker coats in the winter and appeared to enjoy the rain, perhaps fortunate so far north. Fenced in for their own protection from dogs and foxes, the wallabies shared their grazing with Bantam hens. Miller's short article on his wallabies is accompanied by a charming, if blurred, photograph of the happy marsupials lazing on the lawns literally a hop, skip and jump away from Miller's front door.

WOMBAT

Few animals can have inspired such outpourings of poetry, or care, as the unfortunate wombats that shared the garden of the artist Dante Gabriel Rossetti. Not known for his temperance in affection (having a long term affair with Jane Morris, the wife of his close friend and colleague William Morris) Rossetti appears to have been overwhelmed by the charms of the wombat. Wombats were not the first, or only, animals which the artist installed in his one acre gardens at 16 Cheyne Walk, London, having flirted previously with racoons, wallaby, marmots, kangaroos, a Brahmin Bull (zebu), peacocks and armadillos. Wombats, Rossetti declared, were God's most favourite creatures, and co-incidentally, Rossetti's also. Rossetti's wombats were to be the first in the country. He was inspired to record their long anticipated arrival in verse, whilst away at the family seat of Penkill Castle in Scotland:

'Oh, how the family affections combat,
Within the heart, and each hour flings a bomb at
My burning soul! Neither from owl nor from bat
Can peace be gained until I clasp my wombat'.

The arrival of the wombat did not bring the longed for peace, as despite spending long periods asleep, the wombat's waking hours appear to have been dedicated to harassing Rossetti visitors. Whilst sitting for her portrait Mrs Virtue Tebbs was distressed to find the wombat had consumed her straw hat, although whether it was due to form part of the portrait is unknown. Rossetti, by now painfully aware of the precarious nature of wombat health, was distraught, crying out 'Oh poor wombat! It is so indigestible'. On another occasion 'Top', as the first of the two wombats was named, had nibbled a dinner guest's trouser legs, before snuggling up into the large *épergne* on the dinner table, whilst the artist Ruskin had had the indignity of being burrowed into by the wombat whilst holding forth. A description of Rossetti's garden at the time may suggest that there was little to tempt the wombat away from articles of clothing, as although over an acre in size it was said to be in a very neglected condition. Whilst out in the garden the wombat did however make firm friends,

we are told, with the other occupants, in particular finding much in common with the rabbits. Rossetti was not the only one of his circle charmed by the wombats (two were bought in succession) with sketches of the rather ungainly animals being created by Edward Burne-Jones and Bell Scott. Rossetti himself called it 'a joy, a triumph, a delight and a madness' whilst his sister, Christina Rossetti penned an ode to the wombat in Italian which was much appreciated by her brother although seemingly unnoticed by its object: '*uommibatto agil, giocondo che ti sei fatto, liscio e rotondo*'. Rossetti's brother William had a rather more detached viewpoint, describing the wombat as 'an engagingly lumpish quadruped'. Alas, the wombats did not live for long once they had been clasped by the enthusiastic poet and two died in quick succession. A sketch by Rossetti himself shows the emotional artist sobbing over the lifeless (although still rather chubby) form of a wombat with a memorial urn in the background, and the date 6 November 1869. A verse accompanying this touching, if humorous, illustration claims:

I never reared a young Wombat
To glad me with his pin-hole eye,
But when he most was sweet and fat
And tail-less, he was sure to die!

WORM

Most people take worms in the garden for granted, but Charles Darwin wrote a book about the ones in his. Most famous nowadays for his work on the evolution of species, one of Darwin's other main interests in life was the observation of earthworms, and their role in the 'formation of vegetable matter'. Everything about earthworms fascinated Darwin; their digestion, their sense of smell, their lack of eyes (and yet strange ability to detect light), their sex lives, their mental powers, and most importantly, their castings. Darwin realised that it was by the process of millions of earthworms burrowing and producing castings that depths of loamy topsoil were produced. This constant activity by the otherwise relatively unremarkable worm resulted in the incorporation of fresh vegetable matter into soil, and also accounted for the burial of stones, garden paths and even ancient Roman sites. In order to better understand the life of the worm, and its role in burying ancient artefacts, Darwin studied earthworms on various sites near his home at Down House (Kent) measuring how rapidly objects were buried. The garden path which led from the house to the kitchen garden was part of the experiments, and Darwin compared the rate at which his 'own' worms buried the garden path with the rate they buried layers of burnt ash and chalk in the surrounding fields. Darwin's garden-path worms were included in chapter three of his 1881 publication on *The Formation of Vegetable Mould Through the Action of Worms with Observations on their Habits*. Whereas the 'field' worms had buried a chalk layer to a depth of twelve inches over thirty years, Darwin's garden worms only managed to bury his path by an inch, although it seems an unfair competition given that the garden worms had to compete with the efforts of the gardener to keep the path clear. In order to shift such large amounts of soil Darwin realised that the population of worms in a given piece of ground must be enormous. In an average garden of one acre he postulated there must be 53,767 worms, with a total weight of 356 pounds! A comforting thought if one accidentally 'beheads' one whilst weeding. Darwin also set a circular stone slab into the lawn, which he called the 'worm stone'. He instructed his son, Horace Darwin, to take measurements of the undermining action of the worms on this stone. The stone still survives on the northwest edge of the lawn at Down House. A testimony to Darwin's obsession with garden worms.

YAK

Most of the animals introduced into English gardens not only had to suffer the horrors of the English weather but were also deprived of their natural vegetation and habitat. Their owners had most often never set foot in the country from which their exotic animals had originated, and had no idea as to how to replicate the conditions. Warren Hastings on the other hand was more than familiar with the Indian birthplace of the Yaks that he imported onto his Gloucestershire estate. Following financial collapse and the sale of the family estate of Daylesford, Warren Hastings had decided to make a career in the Civil Service. Appointed Governor of Bengal in 1771, he went on to become the infamous Governor General of British India from 1773 until 1784. Returning to Daylesford, with a view

to eventually re-purchasing the estate, he began to transform this small corner of Gloucestershire into the best India had (in his opinion) to offer. The Yaks were forerunners for what Hastings envisaged to be a wave of Indian (or more correctly Tibetan) immigration into England as he strove to introduce a variety of Indian trees and plants onto the estate. He sent to Alipore for seeds of the custard apple, grew Mediterranean and tropical fruit in his greenhouses and attempted, with some success, to introduce lychees from Bengal, which he thought delicious. Instead of oranges the Orangery was rich with grenadillas, lychees, custard apples, alligator pears and mangoes. The plantings in the gardens and park not only feasted his stomach but also assuaged his 'homesickness' for India. If Hastings was momentarily consoled by the site of the majestic yak grazing the home pastures it is doubtful the yaks were so easily fooled as to mistake the rolling Cotswold hills for the

Tibetan mountains. An experimenter in land economics and ecology, Hastings was not averse to sharing round some of his yaks, notably giving a particularly intractable specimen to the famous surgeon John Hunter. Hunter himself had built up a collection of animals (living and dead) to aid in his understanding of anatomy. Hunter's collection was obviously not just a slaughterhouse of experimentation, as the yak lived on at his Earls Court home for eight years, perhaps providing proof of the charge of intractability. Hastings himself referred to the influx of yaks, Asiatic sheep, Bhutan cattle, goats, and Indian plantings as 'ornamental acquisitions' to Daylesford, and only regretted the situation of the house and grounds was such that the family and its acquisitions were rather too secluded and remote for society to appreciate them. Perhaps it was this seclusion that prevented yak keeping catching on in Regency society as no more is heard of them after his death in 1818.

ZEBRA

Queen Charlotte's zebra was the first ever in Britain. Brought from the Cape of Good Hope on the HMS Terpsichore (does this mean it was a terpsichorean zebra?), it was accommodated by Queen Charlotte in a paddock close to her house at Buckingham Gate, where it was greatly admired. A description in the *London Magazine* appears to have seen the animal in the nature of a composite with legs slightly thicker than stags, body as elegant as a racehorse, stripes like a tiger, tail like a lion, and a voice like a common ass. Despite this menagerie of bodily traits, the writer found the animal 'one of the most beautiful creatures in the world' What he failed to find a comparative for was its vicious temper, perhaps brought on by nicotine addiction as its diet apparently consisted of bread, meat and tobacco. Its portrait was also drawn for the *London Magazine*, although the careful depiction of this single example cannot have done much to help their readers envisage the 'most agreeable sight' of 'two or three hundred of them feeding together' recommended in the article. George Stubbs, portrait painter to the nobility, and the nobility's animals painted the zebra's portrait, managing to imbue a sense of the loneliness undoubtedly felt by an animal removed from agreeable companionship: albeit into a royal paddock. Loneliness, or perhaps poor diet, resulted in early death and a second unfortunate was procured. Despite a diet of hay rather than tobacco, this one too developed an unpredictable temperament, choosing as one of his victims the writer and naturalist Oliver Goldsmith. In his 1774 book *An History of the Earth and Animated Nature*, Goldsmith damningly records for posterity both the ill temper and the imperfection of the zebras 'dewlap' or double chin. The moral of the story, never kick your biographer! Worse fates lay in store for the zebras collected for the menagerie in the gardens of Versailles. In an article in the *Avant-Coureur* (a journal for the amateur naturalist of eighteenth century France) the author suggested that more should be done to promote the union of different species of animals in order to create yet more variety of 'nature's operations'. The obvious place to start, the article went on, would be with a 'coupling' of the zebras at Versailles gardens with the asses, mares, and other different quadrupeds. These couplings, the writer imagined, would take place 'without the least trouble'; although the views of the zebra do not seem to have been consulted. Unlike the unfortunately maligned English zebra, its French counterpart was said to be 'the handsomest and most elegantly attired of all quadrupeds', starting a craze for zebra stripes on men's clothing in the 1780s. An *entente cordiale* between Queen Charlotte's zebra and those at Versailles, seems never to have been suggested.

ZEBU

John Hunter, the celebrated eighteenth century surgeon, kept three zebu in his two acre grounds at Earls Court, then a village two miles outside of London. Every Wednesday these Asiatic humped cattle were harnessed to a cart and led from Hunter's country house in Earls Court to the town house in Leicester Square. The large white zebu would lead and the two smaller darker animals would follow. Usually the cart brought fresh vegetables from the gardens at Earls Court, and returned with stable dung. Being a surgeon, however, Hunter held practical anatomy classes, and every so often the debris from the dissecting classes would be carried out in the cart. Care was usually taken to cover the cart well after the revolting load had been placed on it. On one particular day in 1792 the usual carter was absent (dismissed for drunkenness), and the new carter did not realize what load he was carrying, and the resulting need for cover. After loading the 'hampers' from the dissecting rooms onto the buffalo cart, the new carter ('Scotch 'Wolly' as he was known), retired indoors for a drink prior to the journey. Local lads seeing the possibly fruit and vegetable filled cart in the street dared each other to confront the zebu, and started to pry open the hampers only to find the contents rather different than what they expected. A crowd gathered, and a riot broke out. In the melee, a man tried to cut one of the buffalo from its halter, whereupon it trapped its assailant (apparently a hairdresser by trade) to a door by its horns, before running off down Green St and round Leicester Square with the man still attached to the halter. Astoundingly, given the commotion and the damage done, no-one seems to have thought of reporting the incident to the justices and the cart and zebu continued on their usual rounds. What nobody seems to have queried is the fool-hardiness of keeping large Asiatic humped cattle in a small garden in Earls Court. Perhaps the thought of the leeches, lions, leopards and jackals that Hunter also maintained in his domestic establishment, deterred anyone from demurring. This was not the first occasion on which Hunter had had difficulties with the high-spirited zebu. Hunter had had a fine small 'bull' presented to him by Queen Charlotte and this he used to wrestle in play, entertaining himself with its exertions in its own defence. In one of these contests the bull overpowered him and got him down, and had not one of the servants accidentally come by and frightened the beast away, the frolic would probably have cost him his life. Despite his frequent escapades Hunter set a trend in living anatomy collections, and the 1830s saw the anatomist Mr Brookes establish a *vivarium* in his garden in Blenheim St, London, W1. An artificial mound was constructed for the animals' dens very similar to that of Hunter's, although without the gaping crocodile mouth decoration. Here Brookes was content with the smaller animals and birds, such as raccoons, foxes and hawks, perhaps learning a lesson from his predecessor.

ZEBU II

It seems appropriate to close this small collection of enter-taining and unlikely garden pets, and their correspondingly entertaining and eccentric owners, with the zebu kept by Gabriel Rossetti. Encountered already amongst his arma-dillo, peacocks and wombats in that most crowded of west

London gardens, surely his brief, but lively, introduction of a zebu must encapsulate all that is most challenging about introducing pets into gardens. The acquisition of the zebu was, as has so often been the case in this collection, the result of an instant attachment and a passion to possess the creature, notwithstanding the practical difficulties to be expected. Strolling along Cremorene Gardens in 1864, with his brother William, Rossetti was delighted to find a 'beast show' in progress. Entering into the arenas Rossetti was instantly captivated by the large bull zebu (also known as a Brahmin Bull). Its large brown eyes, as others later claimed, reminded him of his lover, Jane Morris. As he could not have Jane at Cheyne Walk, he could at least have the zebu. However gratification was not to be instant, as neither William nor Rossetti had sufficient 'tin' (in their slang) to purchase and lead away the baleful animal. Instead an arrangement was made to come back the next day with £5 as a down-payment, and a further £15 to be paid once the animal was safely ensconced in the garden. Unlike Gabriel Rossetti, his brother William had some sense of practicality, and insisted at least on ascertaining whether the beast was tame, which its then owner assured it was, having impeccable manners. A shed, he added, would be needed for the colder months, but other than that a half-crown a week would be all that would be needed for its upkeep. It being April, the thought of having to install a shed in an already crowded garden in six months hence, did not bother Rossetti, and he begged his brother to acquire the bull for him. A servant called Pope assisted with its collection and installation into the garden, apparently having no difficulty in persuading it through the passageway, where it 'charged at a fine pace' into the garden, and was tied to a tree. Several days passed with Rossetti too busy with commissions to introduce himself to his new pet, and by the time he did so the bull was feeling less than impeccable in its manners. Whether this was due to a lack in its new quarters, or the constant screams of the peacocks who shared the garden with him (and whom William had suggested should be let out in full cry to distract the neighbour's attention from the new arrival), the bull threw a tantrum. Some accounts claimed that Gabriel merely beat a dignified retreat, others that the enraged bull tore up the roots of the tree and actually chased him across the garden. Whichever version is true, Rossetti decided that it would, after all, not be the best of garden pets, with or without eyes like his beloved Jane. After a brief sojourn, during which Rossetti avoided the garden, the zebu was sold on again, hopefully to more paradisiacal pastures.

Bibliography

Acland, A. *A Devon Family: The Story of the Aclands* (Phillimore, 1981)

Ainger, M. *Gilbert and Sullivan* (Oxford University Press, 2002)

Allen, J. *Samuel Johnson's Menagerie: The beastly lives of exotic quadrupeds in the eighteenth century* (The Erskine Press, 2002)

Allen, M. *William Robinson 1838–1935: Father of the English Flower Garden* (Faber and Faber, 1982)

Amateur Menagerie Club Yearbooks 1912, 1913, 1914&1915, 1916, 1920-21, 1922-23, 1926-7

Anon. (dedicated to the Right Hon. Baroness Burdett Coutts) *The Parlour Menagerie* (John Hogg & Co., 1875)

Anstruther, I. *The Knight and the Umbrella: An account of the Eglinton Tournament 1839* (Alan Sutton, 1986)

Baker, A.P. 'Harrison, 'Beatrice Bohun (1892–1965)' In *Oxford Dictionary of National Biography* (OUP, 2004)

Batey, M. *Alexander Pope: The Poet and the Landscape* (Barn Elms, 1999)

Belozerskaya, M. *The Medici Giraffe: and other tales of exotic animals and power* (Little, Brown and Company, 2006)

Bingley, Rev W. *Animal Biography* (3 vols). (London - printed for Richard Phillips, 1805)

Boshier, T. 'Doing it by the Book: the Gibson family gardens at Hill House, Saffron Walden, and the influence of John Claudius Loudon' In Way, T. (ed.) *Paper Landscapes: Archive Based Studies on Historic Gardens and Landscapes in Essex* (Essex Gardens Trust, 2006)

Boyle, C.A. *Servant of the Empire* (Methuen & Co., 2006)

Brown, J. *My Darling Heriott* (Harper Press, 2006)

Buckland, F. *Log-Book of a Fisherman and Zoologist* (Chapman & Hall, 1875)

Buckland, F. *Notes and Jottings from Animal Life* (Smith, Elder & Co., 1882)

Butler, R. 'Ebby, A tame striped hyena' in *The Amateur Menagerie Club Year Book 1914* pp 79-95 (1914)

Canfield, T. 'Modernist Menagerie: Birds Eye at Walton-on-Thames' In *The London Gardener* vol. 3 for 1997–1998 pp17-21 (1998)

Chapman, N. *Deer* (Whittet Books, 1991)

Chapman, N. and Harris, S. *Muntjac* The Mammal Society, London and the British Deer Society (Fordingbridge, 1996)

Chapman, N., Harris, S. and Stanford, A. 'Reeves' muntjac Muntiacus reevesi in Britain: their history, spread, habitat selection and the role of human intervention in accelerating their dispersal' in *Mammal Review* vol. 24, pp 113 - 160. (1994)

Clarke, E. *Hidcote; the Making of a Garden* (Michael Joseph Ltd, 1989)

Clarke, T.H. *The Rhinoceros from Dürer to Stubbs* (Sotheby's Publications, 1986)

Cogan, 'Mrs Squeaks (my spotted hyena)' in *The Amateur Menagerie Club year Book 1913* pp23-29 (1913)

Conway, H. *Public Parks* (Shire, 1996)

Courtney, W. P. 'Heron, Sir Robert, second baronet (1765–1854)', revised H. C. G. Matthew, *Oxford Dictionary of National Biography*, (Oxford University Press, 2004) [http://www.oxforddnb.com/view/article/13091]

Darwin, C. 1881 *The Formation of Vegetable Mould Through the Action of Worms with Observations on their Habits 1881* (Indy 2002)

David, H. *An Historical Account of the Curiosities of London and Westminster* (in 3 vols.) (Printed for J. Newbery, 1765)

Dennis, H.E. 'The Capybara' *The Amateur Menagerie Club Year Book 1913* pp41-47 (1913)

Desmond, R. *The History of the Royal Botanic Gardens Kew* (Harvill Press, 1995)

Devonshire, Duchess of, *The Garden at Chatsworth* (Ted Smart, 1999)

Devonshire, Duchess of, *The Estate: A View from Chatsworth* (Macmillan, 1990)

Dew-Smith, Mrs. *Tom Tug and Others: Sketches in a Domestic Menagerie* (Seeley & Co. 1899)

Dobson, J. *John Hunter* (E & S Livingstone Ltd, 1969)

Dodsley, R. (ed) *Letters Written by the late Right Honourable Lady Luxborough to William Shenstone Esq.* (London, 1775)

English Heritage *The Gardens at Audley End* (English Heritage, 1995)

Evelyn, H. *The History of the Evelyn Family* (Nash, 1915)

Farrar, L. *Ancient Roman Gardens* (Sutton, 1998)

Festing, S. 'Menageries and the landscape garden' In *Journal of Garden History* vol 8, No. 4, Oct-Dec 1988 pp 63-96 (1988)

Finlayson, J. 'John Hunter's Household' In *Br. Med. J* I, 738-740 (1890)

Fish, T.L. *A Guide to Knowle Cottage, the villa of T.L. Fish Esq. Sidmouth* Printed and sold by W.S. Hoyte (Sidmouth, 1848)

Fowler, M. *Blenheim: Biography of a Palace* (Viking, 1989)

Genders, R. *I Bought a Farm* (Littlebury & Co., 1948)

Genders, R. *Wildlife in the Garden* (Faber and Faber, 1976)

Gibson, R. *The Face in the Corner: Animals in Portraits from the Collections of the National Portrait Gallery* (NPG, 1998)

Ginger, A. 'Daylesford House and Warren Hastings' In *Georgian Group Report and Journal,* 1989 pp80–101

Grey, T. *The Garden History of Devon: An illustrated guide to sources* (University of Exeter Press, 1995)

Grey, R. 'The Author of Pinafore: Sir W.S. Gilbert as I Knew Him' In *Century Illustrated* Vol. I xxxiv pp843-850 (1912)

Guilding, R. '"The most Delightful Lounge in the Metropolis": London's Zoological Gardens from 1825-2000' In *The London Gardener* for 1999-2000 vol. 5 pp38-45 (2000)

Harris, C.M. (ed.) *Papers of William Thornton Volume One 1781–1802* (University Press Virginia, 1995)

Harrison, B. (ed. P. Cleveland-Peck), *The Cello and the Nightingales: the autobiography of Beatrice Harrison* (John Murray, 1985)

Hartlib, S. *The Reformed Commonwealth of Bees* (Printed for Giles Calvert, London, 1655)

Heron, R. (2nd ed.) *Notes by Sir Robert Heron* (Groombridge & Son, 1851)

Hibberd, S. *Rustic Adornments for Homes of Taste* (London, 1856)

Hoage, R.J. and Deiss, W. (eds) *New Worlds, New Animals: From Menagerie to Zoological Park in the Nineteenth Century* (John Hopkins University Press, 1996)

Hobbs, A. S. *Beatrix Potter Artist and Illustrator* (Frederick Warne, 2005)

Holmes, C. *Monet at Giverney* (Cassell & Co, 2001)

Howe, B. *Lady with Green Fingers: The Life of Jane Loudon* (Country Life Ltd, 1961)

Hunting, P. 'Dr John Coakley Lettsom, Plant-Collector of Camberwell' In *Garden History* Vol 34 no. 2 (Winter 2006) pp221-235

International Herald Tribune, 5 October 1951

Jamieson, F. 1994 'The Royal Gardens of the Palace of Holyroodhouse, 1500–1603' in *Garden History*, Vol. 22, No. 1 (Summer, 1994), pp. 18-36

Jekyll, G. *Children and Gardens* (Country Life, 1908)

Jekyll, G. *Home and Garden* (Longmans, Green & Co, 1900)

Jekyll, F. and Taylor, G. (eds.) *A Gardener's Testament: A selection of Articles and Notes by Gertrude Jekyll* (Country Life, 1937)

Johnson, W. (ed.) *Gilbert White's Journals* (Routledge & Kegan Paul Ltd, 1931)

Keeling, C.H. *Where the Crane Danced* (Clam Publications, 1985)

Keeling, C.H. *Where the Zebu Grazed* (Clam Publications, 1989)

Keeling, C.H. *Where the Elephant Walked* (Clam Publications, 1991)

Klinkenborg, V *Timothy's Book: Notes of an English Country Tortoise* (Portobello Books, 2006)

Knight, M. *Pets Usual and Unusual* (Routledge & Kegan Paul, 1951)

Knox, T. 'Joshua Brooke's *Vivarium* an Anatomist's Garden in Blenheim St, W1' In *The London Gardener* vol. 3 for 1997-8, pp 30-34 (1998)

Lambton, L. *Beastly Buildings* (Jonathon Cape Ltd, 1985)

Lambton, L. *Lucinda Lambton's Magnificent Menagerie, or Queer Pets and their Goings-On* (Harper Collins, 1992)

LeFanu, W.R. 'John Hunter's Buffaloes' *British. Med. Journal* vol. 2, 574 (1931)

Ledfors, J. 'Notes on the Early History of Kensington Palace Gardens' In *The London Gardener* Vol. 11, 2005-6 (2006)

Lee, R. *Anecdotes of the Habits and Instinct of Animals* (Grant and Griffith, 1852)

Leech, J. 'Mr Brigg's Adventures in the Highlands' *Punch's Almanac* 1861

Le Lièvre, A. *Miss Willmott of Warley Place: her Life and Gardens* (Faber and Faber, 1980)

Lettsom, J.C. *Grove-Hill: An Horticultural Sketch* (London, 1794)

Lettsom, J.C. *Grove-Hill: An Rural and Horticultural Sketch* (London, 1804)

Lettsom, J.C. *Hints Designed to Promote Beneficence, Temperance and Medical Science* (J. Mamman, 1801)

Lockwood, Lady Julia *Instinct; Or Reason? Being Tales and Anecdotes of Animal Biography* 2nd ed. (Reeves and Turner, 1877)

Loudon, J. *The Young Naturalist's Journey* (William Smith, 1840)

Loudon, J. *Domestic Pets Their Habits and Management* (Grant and Griffith, 1851)

Loudon, J. *The Entertaining Naturalist* (newly revised by W.S. Dallas). (Bell & Daldy, 1867)

Loudon, J. *Loudon's Natural History: Popular Description, Tales and Anecdotes of More than Five Hundred Animals* (new edn edited by Dallas, W.S.) (George Bell and Sons, 1889)

Loudon, J. C. *The Suburban Gardener and Villa Companion* (Longman,

Orme, Brown, Green and Longmans, 1838)

Martyn, M. 'An Exile's Dream Realised: Warren Hastings at Daylesford' *Country Life* Jan 23 1975

Massingham, B. *Miss Jekyll: Portrait of a Great Gardener* (David & Charles, 1973)

Massingham, H. *Birds, Dogs and Others : Natural History Letters 'The Spectator'* (T.Fisher Unwin Ltd, 1921)

McCarthy, S. and Gilbert, M. *The Crystal Palace Dinosaurs* (The Crystal Palace Foundation, 1994)

Miller, O. *Queer Pets and Their Doings* (English edition) (J.F. Shaw & Co, 1882)

Morris, S. et al, *Charles Darwin at Down House* (English Heritage, 1998)

Mowl, T. *Historic Gardens of Gloucestershire* (Tempus, 2002)

National Trust *Killerton House and Garden* (National Trust)

National Trust *Beatrix Potter: Her Art and Inspiration* (National Trust, 2006)

Nissenson, M. and Jonas, S. *The Ubiquitous Pig* (Weidenfeld and Nicolson Ltd, 1993)

O'Regan, H. 'From Bear Pit to Zoo' In *British Archaeology* Issue 68, December 2002

Pedrick, G. *Life With Rossetti: or No Peacocks Allowed* (Macdonald & Co., 1964)

Pepys, S. 1970-83 *The Diary of Samuel Pepys: A new and complete transcription* (Latham, R and Mathews, W eds.) 11 vols. (Bell)

Pevsner, N. *The Buildings of England: Surrey* (Penguin, 1962)

Piebenga, S. 'The nineteenth-century aviary and zoo at Waddesdon Manor, Buckinghamshire' Forthcoming 2007 *Historic Gardens Review*

Pitt, F. 'My Pet Badgers' in *The Amateur Menagerie Club Year Book 1913* pp 53-63 (1913)

Pitt, F. *Meet Us in the Garden* (Lutterworth, 1946)

Pitt, F. *My Squirrels* (Country Life, 1954)

Pitt, F. *Country Years* (George Allen & Unwin Ltd, 1961)

Plomer, W. ed. Kilvert's Diary 1870–1879 (Diary entry 16th August 1872) (Bracken Books, 1986)

Pope, A. 'From Bounce to Fop: An Heroick Epistle from a Dog at Twickenham to a Dog at Court' In Ault. N. and Butt, J (eds.) *Alexander Pope Minor Poems* p57-64 (Methuen, 1954)

Porter, M.R. and Davenport, O. *Scotsmen in Buckskin: Sir William Drummond Stewart and the Rocky Mountain Fur Trade* (Hastings House, 1963)

Potter, J. *Lost Gardens* (Channel 4, 2000)

Qvist, G. *John Hunter 1728–1793* (William Heinemann Medical Books Ltd, 1981)

Richards, A. *Portraits of the Curious Exotic Birds which formerly composed the Osterly Menagerie* (Victoria Press, 1846)

Ritvo, H. *The Animal Estate: The English and Other Creatures in the Victorian Age* (Harvard University Press, 1987)

Roberts, V. *Poultry for Anyone* (Whittet Books, 1997)

Robbins, L.E. *Elephant Slaves and Pampered Parrots; Exotic Animals in Eighteenth-Century Paris* (The John Hopkins University Press, 2002)

Rohde, E.S. *The Story of the Garden* (Medici, 1932)

Rolfe, W.D. 'A Stubbs Drawing Recognised' In *The Burlington Magazine,* vol. 125, No.969 (Dec. 1983) pp738-741

Rothschild, Dame M. *Dear Lord Rothschild: Birds, Butterflies and History* (Hutchinson, 1983)

Rothschild, Dame M. *The Butterfly Gardener* (Michael Joseph, 1983)

Sackville-West, V. *Faces: Profiles of Dogs* (Harvill Press, 1961)

Shaw, G. *General Zoology or Systematic Natural History, Mammalia,* 2 vols. (Davison, 1800)

Soper, E.G. *Muntjac* (Longmans, Green and Co., 1969)

Strong, L. 'American Indians and Scottish Identity in Sir William Drummond Stewart's Collection' In *Winterthur Portfolio,* Vol. 35, No. 2/3 (Summer-Autumn 2000) p127–155

The Perambulator 'Don't Eat the Ducks: Transgression in Public Parks' In *The London Gardener* Vol. 11 2005-6

The Studio Magazine *Modern Gardens British and Foreign* 1926-27

Thomas, W.K. 'His Highness' Dog at Kew' In *College English* Vol. 30, No. 7 (April 1969) pp581-586

Tipping, H. Avray 'Hidcote Manor Garden' In *Country Life,* vol. lxvii, 1930, pp286-94; and vol. lxviii pp231-3

Topsell, E. *The Historie of Four Footed Beastes* London (1607 and later edition 1658 revised and corrected by John Rowland MD)

Turner, M. *Eltham Palace* (English Heritage, 2005)

Wain, L. 'The Hon. Walter Rothschild's Pets' in *The Windsor Magazine* December 1895 Vol 2. No. 12

Walker, N. 'Monkey Mania' in *The Amateur Menagerie Club Year Book* 1926-7 pp. 65-77

Way, T. (ed.) *Paper Landscapes: Archive Based Studies on Historic Gardens and Landscapes in Essex* (Essex Gardens Trust, 2005)

Way, T. *Histon Manor, Cambridgeshire* (Private Report held by author and clients, 2000)

Way, T. *Virgins, Weeders and Queens: A History of Women in the Garden* (Sutton, 2006)

Wilson, V. 'My Chameleon' in *The Amateur Menagerie Club Year Book 1912* pp 93-97 (1912)

White, G. *The Natural History and Antiquities of Selborne, in the County of Southampton* (London, 1788)

Wood, Rev. T. *Petland Revisited* (Longmans, Green & Co., 1884)

Wood, Rev. T. *Out-of-the-Way Pets and other papers* (Fredk. Sherlock, London, 1896)

Zoological Society *The Gardens and Menagerie of the Zoological Society Delineated* (Thomas Tegg, Cheapside, 1830)

WEBSITES:

Pelicans:
www.bbc.co.uk/1/hi/england/london/6083468.stm

Père David's Deer
http://www.ultimateungulate.com

Presidential Pets:
http://www.simplyfamily.com/display.cfm?articleID=presidential_pets.cfm
http://presidentialpetmuseum.com/whitehousepets

Purple Swamphen
http://en.wikipedia.org/wiki/PurpleSwamphen

Raccoon
Time magazine: 4 July 1927
http://www.time.com/time/magazine/article/0,9171,785829-2,00.html
http://www.davidpietrusza.com/coolidge-pets.html